Making Yo
Work

Making Your Work
Work

Everyday performance revolution

Jan Gillett

infinite**ideas**

First published in 2014 by
Infinite Ideas Limited
36 St Giles
Oxford
OX1 3LD
United Kingdom
www.infideas.com

A CIP catalogue record for this book is available from the British Library
ISBN 978-1-908984-20-3

Designed by Nick Clarke
Typeset by Nicki Averill
Printed in Spain

'*Making your work work* should be required reading for any manager who wants to guide and strengthen an organization's processes and practices. This book is an extraordinary gift to any manager who wants to excel as an informed leader capable of wise behavior leading to practical results. It explains the unique pressures that managers face and sets forth concrete steps for handling these difficult challenges. Gillett tells managers how to think about their organization, how to identify compelling issues, and how to make sound choices leading to effective action.'

Elaine Johnson PhD., author of *A Beginner's Guide to the Brain*

'This reading offers practical and useful insight on how to truly operate as an outstanding Process Manager'

James Horton, EMEA Lean Director, GSC Healthcare – General Electric, UK

'Here's a book that combines the step-by-step methods of initiating improvement activity with very practical insights into the human aspects of how to make the change work and last. It balances the short term needs of a manager to show quick progress, together with building the muscle needed to sustain improvements ... a must-read for any manager of people starting out on this exciting journey.'

J Ravikant, Head of Corporate TQM at SRF Limited, India

'Excellence made practical and plain easier. In my experience getting on with excellence is about making theory and methods easily accessible and understood from the outset, at all levels of the organisation. This requires relevant examples and good storytelling wrapped around them, and Jan does that really well. This makes optimal reading before proceeding on a process excellence journey.'

Adam Gade, Managing Partner, A&D resources, Former CIO, Maersk Line, AP Moller Maersk Group, Denmark

'Discovering PDSA and the System of Profound Knowledge explained in such a usable format has enabled change management programmes to be referenced to a 'back to basics' approach. The examples identified in Ann's Story have been extremely beneficial in helping the wider organisation realise they are not that different. Leadership quickly came to understand that they needed to learn about how to change, before they could begin to fully understand the 'end to end' processes involved.'

Senior Engineer in British Armed Forces

To Eleanor, Charly, Alex, Charlotte and Rachel. Hoping this helps them as the twenty-first century unfolds as it did for me in the twentieth.

Contents

Foreword

Professor Tom Johnson

When you think of the advice most consultants give to managers, probably the first thing that comes to mind is their promise that a new set of generic tools or practices will produce far better results than any previous or current tools and practices have done. In fact the idea that tools and practices are the key to a manager's success is widely held not only among business consultants, but also among business educators in universities. It is perhaps surprising, then, to see a consultant tell managers that better results can be had by adopting new thinking about how work should work, rather than just introducing new tools and techniques into an unexamined work environment. However, that is exactly what Jan Gillett is telling managers in *Making Your Work Work*.

Gillett's ideas about how to 'make your work work better' are firmly grounded in W. Edwards Deming's System of Profound Knowledge and are corroborated by the exceptional performance of organisations that manage their work according to Deming's principles. Those organisations include several Japanese companies – especially Toyota – that Deming advised in the 1950s and a number of companies coached in Deming's principles over the past 30 years by Process Management International Limited, the consulting firm co-founded by Jan Gillett. In *Making Your Work Work*, Gillett shows how a manager succeeds by instilling every facet of a company's work with those principles, not by imposing abstract generic methods and targets on the work from the outside. Indeed, the story Gillett weaves so skillfully through the chapters of this book gives readers an exceptional understanding of Deming's unique and powerful message.

A key insight managers should draw from this book is a firm understanding that long-term success in business is not a result of solving a succession of technical problems. Rather, it grows from a process of building and nurturing patterns of interdependent relationships among people who engage in gainful employment serving customers as well as earning profit. In that process, guided by Deming's principles, financial results are not an end that justifies any means, no matter how destructive to society or nature. Instead, the process – the means – transforms work into results, including fair and just financial profit, that enrich the common good.

H. Thomas Johnson

H. Thomas Johnson is the author of *Profit Beyond Measure: Extraordinary Results through Attention to Process and People*, which was awarded the 2001 Shingo Prize For Excellence in Manufacturing Research. For many years he was Professor of Business Administration at Portland State University in Oregon. In 2007 he received the Deming Medal in recognition of lifetime achievement, from the American Society for Quality.

Epiphanies

Then I felt like some watcher of the skies, when a new planet
swims into his ken.
John Keats, poet, 1795–1821

An epiphany is an experience of sudden and striking realization
(Wikipedia). You never quite recover from an epiphany; you can't get
back to your state of mind beforehand. Most of us have a few of them
through our lives; some of them lead to life-changing decisions.

Epiphany # 1. Revolutionary ideas

Summer 1988 in Leicestershire, England. I glanced around the boardroom
at my directors; doubt was written on every face. I had been managing
director for a year or so and was new to their industry; they had been
running the business, more or less successfully, for many years. Out at the
front was University of Nottingham statistician, Dr Henry Neave, a few
minutes into the life story of an 87-year-old American called Dr Deming.
No wonder they were shifting in their seats.

They were at the meeting because I had insisted on it. Henry had
asked for two hours, an unheard-of break in the daily routine. And I had
insisted because the Ford Motor Company, our second largest customer,
had told us to adopt the 'Deming Approach to Quality Management' and
the first step turned out to be a request for their purchasing manager
Trevor Cordwell, and Henry, to address my board.

Trevor spoke briefly. That was OK; they knew his kind, but then he
handed over to Henry. So here we all were, waiting for him to get to the
point, whatever it was, and prove that he had something worthwhile to
say, and then to tell us what to do.

We had not heard of Total Quality Management, still less of Dr
Deming, but we were all aware that there was something special going on
in Japan, and we had witnessed the extraordinary growth of the Japanese
car companies in our home market. The media had told us their success
was due to subsidies, cheap labour, exchange rates, being Japanese, not
being unionised, and something definitely unfair, whatever it was. But

Nissan had just started manufacturing in the UK with a new plant built on time, on cost, and with a new model just as reliable as the old one. This was unheard of; it all seemed like magic to most of us, and was still not something that we could aspire to doing. And how could an ancient American have anything to do with it?

Over those two hours Henry covered a lot of ground. Deming had apparently been in on the birth of something called statistical process control in the 1930s, and was regarded as the father of the Japanese quality revolution. He'd been deeply involved with the whole Japanese renaissance since 1950, even been presented with some kind of medal by their Emperor, no less. He had been rediscovered in the US in 1979, and had since worked with Ford and many other big names. This was credibility indeed and I knew we needed some of this magic. But what was the magic?

A particularly striking moment – my epiphany – came when Henry described Dr Deming's logic that if you ran good processes that were focussed on the customer, you would win their loyalty at less cost than the old ways, and hence gain a greater market share at a better price. This is what the successful Japanese companies in the motor and other industries had apparently been doing. I had spent more than twenty years in environments that focussed on the owners, treated customers with disrespect, and tried to cut costs and get away with it. They had not been rewarding environments in which to work, and apart from lucky times when we could dominate customers they were not very successful either. It had never occurred to me that there was an alternative – making the work work properly and getting lower costs – because no one else was any different. But here was a plausible principle underpinning the relentless Japanese advances in the motor industry that I had watched for years.

There were many more striking points in the two hours – too many to recall at the time. There were fourteen points for managers and five deadly diseases, interesting but not specific enough for us to act. But several board members thought that we should try to do this – helped not a little by Trevor's presence, of course. They seemed to be ready to change as we were very unhappy with our performance for Ford, and very attracted to becoming more like Nissan or Toyota. We agreed at the end that we would investigate 'adopting the Deming Approach'.

So after the meeting I sat with Henry and Trevor and said 'What do we do next?' There was a torrent of questions: 'Who can I visit and copy?' 'Who can teach us?' 'Where do we start?'

'You have to start with learning,' they said; there was no instant solution, no point trying to copy. This was shocking to me. I had been given a tantalising glimpse of nirvana, but the door was being slammed in my face. In fact, there wasn't even a door; we had been given some kind of aerial view with no way to get our feet on the ground.

To cut a long story short I did learn, much more than I ever thought was possible for, after all, I had risen to MD positions at a young age and been successful. I met Dr Deming, eventually attending three of his famous Four-Day Seminars, and was drawn into his approach, which was also outlined in his book *Out of the Crisis*. But he had no prescription; we had to work it out for ourselves – which we did to some extent over the next two years or so, making some big mistakes but learning from them, and achieving some huge and unexpected gains.

Epiphany # 2. Leading the application is uniquely rewarding

A factory visit in 1989, a few weeks after a second attempt at comprehensive reworking of the layout, accelerating the flow, reducing work in progress, saving space. The first version had been an embarrassment with poor communication and therefore misunderstandings and customer problems. From across the production line came a call: 'Excuse me, boss...' Oh boy, what's this? The line workers don't usually call out to the visiting MD. 'Excuse me, I'd like to thank you, Mr Gillett.' Thank me? This was a first. What on earth for? 'I'd like to thank you, this new system lets us get things through well ahead of schedule, and it's better for the customers and easier for us. We know it's not been easy and we weren't keen at first, but it's great, so thank you.' 'Well, thanks, guys,' I said, 'and there'll be more to come so I look forward to coming back again.'

Readers will know that such conversations are rare indeed. As MD I never got a thank you for a wage increase, or pretty much anything in fact. So this experience was inspiring, the first of many that have carried me forward over the often frustrating decades of leading and facilitating transformation. We had indeed saved more costs than we expected, we stood years of received wisdom about space utilisation on its head, and we reduced missing products by over tenfold. Amazing: all this, and enthusiasm from shop floor staff and supervision.

Over the next two years we had achieved many more gains, having developed a programme across the business of two thousand or so people, even though we stumbled many times on the way. We discovered that making the work flow properly led to great things, but that it was not at all easy, demanding many changes of culture and behaviour, especially at the top. There were no short cuts. It was so powerful and people would evidently need experienced help, so I decided to change career, to become a consultant in business improvement and transformation. Having been to many conferences by then I had no doubt that Dr Deming's approach was the right way to go, being based upon culture, thinking and principles, and not just tools and techniques. What I couldn't be sure of was how to facilitate as a consultant rather than lead as a CEO.

Epiphany # 3. A shared approach revolutionises supply chain relationships

Some years later, at a conference centre near Coventry, England, two years into a variability reduction programme across the supply chain of an automotive group that had more than a hundred suppliers. We had worked with top management, supported many projects, trained many people. We had brought together 150 or so managers and improvement staff from production, design and procurement in the customer, and from sales and manufacturing in the suppliers. They shared their experiences and learning about reducing variation and making many tangible gains, in Deming's common language. This had led to so many benefits; they had increased reliability, saved money and time, and reduced confusion. But the most positive of all were the connections that they had been able to make across their complex system as they used that common language to examine how their work actually worked and how to make it better by reducing variation. We heard of meetings to resolve problems involving production and engineering staff from both customer and supplier, where for the first time anyone could remember they would use the one methodology, the same approach to data and decision making. Some were quite emotional about the experience – and that brought about an epiphany for many of them, and confirmation of the validity of our approach to me.

We built our company into a successful global operator, covering a huge range of organisation sectors and applications. Our clients experienced countless personal epiphanies, some that they delight in sharing years later.

Epiphany # 4. Making the work work in this way is global

A motorcycle factory in Bangalore, India. The company had won the prestigious Deming Prize for their strategy, performance and quality, and we were visiting with some of the Japanese academics and consultant friends who had worked with them. But this was no 'royal visit'. We were being guided by the production managers, confident in their ability to respond to any question about their methods. I asked a foreman on the gear-machining line about process capability: the performance of the routine production in comparison to its targets. He readily took me to the workplace display and talked me through their control charts, able to explain how they showed the stability of the process, how it influenced their decisions, and how the graph demonstrated that less than one in a million would be outside the specification. This is at least the equal of any sophisticated western factory. Their capability was built on culture, participation, education and leadership, not on capital investment and top-down control. The light in his eyes spoke volumes.

Epiphany # 5. When everyone, everywhere, gets the message and uses it every day, the sky is the limit

Downtown Manila, Philippines, a large service office for our client, a global shipping company. Two thousand staff work on the mass transactions involved in getting millions of containers from their loading point to their destination via continually changing routes, ships, ports and so on. It may be a service department, but it's manufacturing on a mind-boggling scale. They take the information inputs and make better information outputs, many thousands of finished 'products' every day, whose characteristics are no less vital than an aircraft component for all that they are invisible. Two supervisors of their work groups talk me through the workplace display showing process flow, the control charts showing the variation of time, rework and so on. There's not a specialist process facilitator in sight, and the knowledge and enthusiasm in the workplace was palpable. Their epiphany was the way in which our approach gave them the confidence to make local decisions and the evidence of how such decisions work out in practice. Wow! A long way, in every sense, from the UK in 1988.

You would never know it, but the picture in Manila was just the tip of an iceberg. Their company had saved hundreds of millions of dollars across the world by understanding how their administration work worked, and transforming its effectiveness: focussing on the customer, redefining the purpose, getting the flow lined up, and reducing the variation and waste. This effectiveness had delivered the efficiencies that they had demanded, and failed to realise, for years.

Enough epiphanies; you get the message. Our experience stretches back to the early 80s, experience of first- and second-hand application of the principles together with methodologies that we have developed under the extreme pressure of client application.

- We can say with absolute certainty that you can rely on the principles in this book if you use them properly – no matter what your work environment, culture or geography.
- The methodologies that structure the application, from strategy to daily work, are tremendously robust when used properly.
- The dozens of tools provide insight and discipline whenever they are used properly.

You will have noticed, and maybe been irritated by, the triple reference to 'used properly'. As with any other principle or tool in life, from the ten commandments to a lawn mower or a golf club, if you don't pay attention to instructions and apply them properly, they don't work well. In fact, they can do more harm than good.

As I have learned how to apply the ideas and methods better, I have often wished that I had known about them in my early career. This book summarises how the everyday manager, working in everyday circumstances, can learn to use them increasingly well – right from the start of their career through to becoming a top manager because of their effectiveness in making their work work properly.

Just one more thing. The principles and so on only work when they are actually used. Just thinking they might be a good idea doesn't help at all. If you are a manager it's your job to lead and apply them, and this means sticking your neck out sometimes. You don't get to be the best without being different, but being this different is the lowest risk you will have the chance to take. I hope you find it as rewarding as we have.

Introduction

Nothing will ever be attempted if all possible objections must first be overcome.
Dr Johnson, 1759

Never doubt that a small group of thoughtful, committed, citizens can change the world. Indeed, it is the only thing that ever has.
Margaret Mead, anthropologist, 1901–78

As you progress through the book you will find many opportunities to apply what you read about. At the risk of repetition, do take them. This is learning by doing and it's the only way to make the work work better, rather than just thinking or talking about it.

Ann's story

The label on the desk said 'customer service manager', so she walked round and sat down. That was the title on the appointment letter so this must be it; the others seemed to be hot desks for anyone to use. In five minutes the IT manager would be coming to set up her account, give her access to the files and the calendar, and a phone of course – and then she would have an hour before the first operations team meeting, the first chance to meet her peers and see how her new boss worked. According to the note she had been sent, tomorrow would be the weekly conference call with her supervisors, including the agency in Mumbai that handled complaints, and then there would be a planning meeting only two days later.

Although Ann had been flattered to get this job she was not quite convinced she had what it would take, not having been in charge of many people before. She had seen others buckle under such demands, and she had not much training beyond team building and interviewing skills. Decisions would be required, costs had to be cut, but response times had to improve and staff morale was said not to be good. All this had been made clear at the interview.

> She laid her personal tablet and phone on the desk, looked around
> the department for a moment and opened the top drawer, interested to
> see an envelope addressed to her. Before she could open it, there was a
> movement in front of her. She invited the IT manager to sit down…

There's only one chance to make the first impression

The first day in a new job as a manager; countless thousands have
experienced it, with infinite variations of circumstances and characters.
Some people settle in quickly, apparently blessed by innate ability and
possibly luck, perhaps taking advantage with another rapid promotion.
Some fall by the wayside in a few months, unhinged by the pressure,
making decisions that lead to failures or not making any decisions and
losing credibility. The majority get by, not too well if not too badly, fixing
problems as they come, not presiding over disasters, looking busy but not
making much real progress. Nonetheless a promotion may still happen
– after all, there's always a demand for firefighters – but then their stress
level may be heightened further. Most new managers start out hoping
to make the underlying work work better, not just to deal with crises,
but few are confident they know how to keep it that way. Consistency
is elusive for most. We routinely see such hopeful but slightly unsure
people in our work, both in our clients and amongst the many individuals
who attend our training courses. We also encounter those who give the
appearance of being on top of everything but who preside over a reactive,
stressed operation.

For the truth is that most work does not actually work very well. The
majority of our encounters with the results of other people's work leave
us at least mildly dissatisfied, whether from hassles with changing phone
providers to cancellations of appointments, faulty products, abrupt
personal interactions and a seemingly endless array of aggravations
in financial services. You can see these problems illustrated in the
help columns of many newspapers with some organisations regularly
appearing there, often resistant to making amends at all. Others only
seem to respond to contact with their press office, which can somehow
unlock solutions not available by regular channels.

We are all the recipients of such failures, but it's equally likely that in
our everyday jobs we can be contributing to reciprocal mediocrity, in

truth letting others down as much as they fall short with us. The numbing effect of all this noise is often turned into an almost general anaesthesia by reluctance to listen to the customers themselves, and by department managers having to manipulate their data (financial or otherwise) to make results seem OK. The world can revolve around the budgets, the inspections, the management meetings. The adding value and customer-facing work can take second place, with not much ingenuity left after negotiating the corporate obstacle course.

Hence most managers have a high threshold of pain. They've learned not to expect perfection, and when they don't get it they don't make a fuss; maybe they don't even notice it. And thus they don't aspire to delivering it either. The more senior they are, the less they seem aware of the everyday realities.

How ready are you to change?

We hope that you have a lower threshold of pain, which is why you have picked up this book. We hope that you would like to do things differently: things that would make your work work better, perhaps by better serving your customers or lowering costs or whatever is important. Maybe you have heard that both can be achieved at once, but organisations which achieve that are clearly rather special and you are not sure what's involved. You wonder how much you might have to change.

In order to take the risks involved with changing any behaviour, it's necessary to have sufficient dissatisfaction with how things are at present. By bothering to read this book you may already be fed up enough to qualify.

However, frustration is not enough in its own. It's also necessary to have some better way in mind, one that is attractive enough to care about and reasonably well enough defined to be doable. Hopes and dreams are all very well, but miracles are not to be relied upon. We hope that as you progress through the book you will be motivated to make those personal changes that will mean your department delivers better quality at lower cost, and with more job satisfaction all round.

This better way is clearly not common, but one place you can experience it is by looking closely at the world's motor industry. In the twenty-first century, if we have the money we take it for granted that we can buy one of the most complicated mass-produced creations that humanity has so far conceived of – a motor car – at a relative price that is cheaper than ever, and that it will work. Every car is made up of thousands of components. Even the cheapest car has the computing power of a dozen laptops; they show ingenuity and even beauty in design, and will work for years with minimum skill in operating and virtually no maintenance. It's amazing when you stop and think about it, and cars are a big contrast with many other products.

Not every auto manufacturer has achieved all this, but those who have practise the methodologies described in this book, and more. Their culture is built on much the same foundations or principles we describe. We may worry that the motor industry consumes too much space and too many resources and that its products pollute our atmosphere, but that should not take away from the astonishing achievements in what the industry makes and how it does so. In Europe and North America in the 1970s it was expected that a new car would break down in its first year, perhaps several times. The Japanese car makers built their market share on being amazingly (so we thought) reliable as well as cheaper. We now take this for granted.

Many Japanese auto companies have readily shared their approach to this revolution, and thousands of organisations around the world, across virtually every economic and public sector, have tried to emulate them. Many western-owned auto companies have greatly improved as a result, but most Japanese makes are still ahead, having improved even more from their head start. Few others have succeeded completely, with many different reasons for falling short. That's often a consequence of regarding the challenge as a technical one, emphasising tools and transactions at the expense of principles and methodologies, particularly those affecting people. It's also necessary to persist for many years if the approach is to become deeply rooted.

We don't want to paint these auto companies as paragons of virtue; after all, they are, in the end, complex human systems led by fallible people. But over many decades they have achieved astonishing standards, and we all can learn more by studying their success factors (what we could be doing) rather than poring over the failure of more mundane examples nearer home (what we should not be doing). They can provide the basis of a vision to aspire to.

What we are trying to accomplish
Our vision is that every manager at work is aware of the 'essential oils' that lubricate the achievements of Toyota, Honda, Nissan and other

companies that have lived this way of working for decades. Our learning in these foundations and in which methodologies are useful, with or without the tools, since the 1980s has led us to those you find in the next few chapters: the relatively small number of key methodologies that provide the context for the tools, however many of those you may personally know. We hope you will join us in learning how to set up the environment and use it. This will give you the chance to make the most of that first impression in a new role. And, if actually you've been around a while, the first chance to make a new impression!

The principles: Deming's System of Profound Knowledge

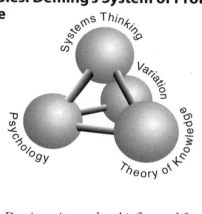

Dr W Edwards Deming witnessed and influenced first-hand the first mass-production economy in the 1930s and the extraordinary achievements of US military manufacturing in the 1940s. He was involved from the very start in the Japanese renaissance from 1950, gaining awards and deep respect in Japanese society. From 1980 he was asked to advise US industry and then do the same in Europe and Asia. He developed the 'System of Profound Knowledge' in the late 1980s as a result of this practice across the world over six decades. We met him at the end of his long and active life, and were deeply moved by his personal insight as well as his technical mastery.

It is worth remarking on this evolutionary development process of the System of Profound Knowledge. It was not some bright young academic's model; it was the result of sixty years' thought and experience across the world. Since the late 1980s we have used it both in running our business and with our clients, and found it necessary and complete – a unique way of thinking about any organisation, on any scale, anywhere. We know of no similar approach.

Our model for learning – the 'Plan Do Study Act' Cycle

We will be referring to the PDSA, or Deming, Cycle throughout the book. This is the learning model that should guide all your decisions, and is a context for all the methodologies. It is a version of the scientific method which evolved over hundreds of years and has led to countless discoveries about the natural world and the universe. The scientific method lies behind the technologies and achievements that we are amazed by, just as much as those we later take for granted, and it is the basis of our material aspirations for the future. Only by its stimulation of relentless innovation and experiment can we hope to come up with the new products and services demanded by changing circumstances.

Working with the PDSA Cycle enables everyone to learn and apply new thinking in a real-world environment. It is not a magic bullet, and using it will rarely provide certainty, but it does provide a process and language that all can share. We use it either in stages or as a whole cycle throughout the book, and expand on the explanation in the Appendices.

The structure of this book

The sequence of *Making Your Work Work* runs from taking on a new job or rethinking an existing one, and working to improve how it works without having to do a training course first. Just as Isaac Newton created a revolution in productivity in the English Royal Mint in the late seventeenth century (see Chapter 7), you will see that it's the overall approach that counts: principles guide thinking, methodologies provide structure, tools reveal the details.

Applying Dr Deming's principles will work for you too. I wish you good fortune in applying them.

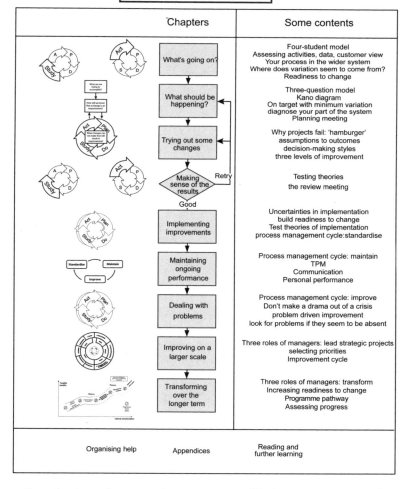

In order to make some plans to test possible improvements, we first need to find out what is going on. So let's get started!

1 Find out how the work is working

The beginning of knowledge is the discovery of something
we do not understand.
Frank Herbert, US author, 1920–86

Ann's story

Ten days later, Ann got off the plane and headed for the car park, looking for the local service manager. This was the first time she had left head office in this new job, and she hoped to find a little more clarity out here near the customers, away from the obsessions with forecasts, budgets, complaints, staff problems and so on which had emerged relentlessly since that first morning. Everyone around her seemed to be expecting decisions, commitments, miracles even. She knew that her predecessor had not been very highly regarded, but did not think that so much could be going wrong just because of a pedestrian manager. She suspected that there were deeper issues, but how to find out what they were, how to hold off making rushed judgements – that was not at all clear.

The envelope in her desk had contained a sweepstake with several estimates of how many months she would survive in her new role. It was, of course, unclear who had left it there, but the track record was not good. There had been four incumbents in the previous five years, and estimates of her survival in this sweep varied between six and eighteen months. Considering this was her first big job, such speculation was no joke. She had left the security of her previous employer, with plenty of backup and a pension, and this new company was smaller, with fewer places to hide if things didn't work out. Still, the IT guy had said there was lots to get at easily, people just hadn't been listening and she should look at the cheque payment procedure.

So it had therefore been with a little trepidation that she had proposed to her boss that she take the first month to get out and see what was happening before committing to any decisions. He had somewhat reluctantly agreed to postpone the planning meeting, but had promised to listen to her conclusions with an open mind.

> Here was the car, her first encounter with the real work, what would it show, where would it lead? She opened the door and climbed in, leaning across to shake the hand of the service manager.

Study – what's going on?

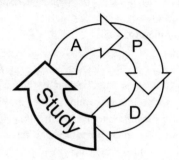

Any reader who has taken on a new job will recognise how difficult it is to get the real picture of what is actually happening. People will tell you what they think is going on, but what they say will vary, perhaps wildly. You may find work instructions, flowcharts, customer surveys, data, of course, but 'facts' will be in short supply. Hopes, dreams, disappointments, pride, conscience, politics, are just some of the intangibles that will filter the reality. They are inescapable aspects of human behaviour.

In particular, several people are likely to say something like 'this is a simple job, but we overcomplicate it; just do this, or stop doing that'. If only that were true. Few jobs really are simple, and many are the ways to overcomplicate even those that are. Let's try to get to the essence of what is happening.

> If a tree falls in the forest when no one is around, does it make a sound?
> **Attributed to George Berkeley, 1710**

This ancient riddle has many possible answers (just look it up on Wikipedia), but in the forest, or maybe more of a jungle, of your work a few of them are highly relevant. Across your department and amongst those influenced by it, and those which influence it, lots of things are going on. Proverbial trees are growing, falling over, being cut down, leaning on others. Some are resisting the weather no matter what, others are ready to tumble at the next puff of wind. But who hears them if they do fall? And what sense do they make of the noise if they do?

As with the falling trees, only a small proportion of the events in your function will register with anyone apart from the immediate participants, who may include customers, of course. From our experience at the start of our assignments, we see that even apparently tangible data may not be representative or accurate. Most events are not being measured. For instance, a call centre manager may be able to see staff at work, check when they arrived or last went to the toilet. But how can that manager possibly know why every order was lost or won, even if they do watch and every word is recorded? The great majority of work is invisible to the bosses to most intents and purposes. Operations carried out by home workers, night shifts, delivery drivers, technical support, production staff, these are the equivalents to the trees falling – or not – in the forest with no one there. We all know people who behave in one way when they think they are being observed and in another when not, including ourselves, so making sense of it all is not easy.

Let's get back to the three-hundred-year-old question about trees and noise. For our purposes the answer is that every tree must make a sound, but no one can be sure when, how loudly, why and with what consequences, and so on. So it goes at work. In your area of responsibility you can never be sure about most individual events. Data about events are abstractions, not 'facts'; they are imperfect reflections of reality and should only be used in decision making with great care. Spending time poring over spreadsheets will not show how the work is working. You need to learn the flow of how it actually works and thus be more confident about what might be influencing the data.

Hence you should approach the subject of this chapter – what is going on – with caution. You can get a feeling for it, one good enough to take some decisions about possible changes to test, but don't hope to be certain and beware of those who assert that they do know what to change. As we have already said, much data that exists is not reliable, and not used very well. Many decisions are taken without good data and little context; we call this 'tampering'. This needs to change. Only data that are useful should be collected, and decisions should refer to data in the context of the process that generates it.

This uncertainty is one way in which human organisations (systems) have much in common with natural systems. Hence your approach will have more parallels with a natural scientist than you probably expected, and we can learn many lessons from their approach to experiments.

Assessing the prospects

There are a lot of ways to build your impressions, alternative models that suit some people more than others in different situations. One size does not fit all. Try some of them initially, then return to the chapter later on and consider others that could be useful too.

At the end of the initial study you need to be able to say 'My assessment is that this is how well I think we are doing, this is why, and here are some aspects I am going to concentrate on to improve matters.' You will thus initially be interested in what is happening, how well it works, how problems are responded to, and what the atmosphere is like. You want evidence that indicates the prospects so that you can develop theories of cause and effect.

> Where observation is concerned, chance favours only the
> prepared mind.
> **Louis Pasteur, scientist, 1822–95**

The Four-Student Model

In thinking about the kind of evidence, consider the prospects for a class of four students. Note, we are interested in their prospects, not in judging their past. They have taken their exams, doing well or not so well, and have followed the teaching process or not, i.e. been diligent or neglectful in attending class. This presents us with four possibilities:

Student	Result	Attended the class?	Comments
A	Passed	Yes, diligently	Good prospects
B	Passed	No, was absent	Lucky – this time!
C	Failed	Yes, diligently	Hopeless (student or class!)
D	Failed	No, was absent	Some hope; try attending!

This model was first developed by Professor Noriaki Kano.

Now, most of us have seen something of this in our education. Some people sailed through exams without effort, whilst others who studied hard failed.

And vice versa. As far as the examination system is concerned it is only interested in results. It has done its job if it has separated 'good' from 'bad', regardless of reasons.[1] It does not discriminate between students who learned the methods and can explain them, and those who can remember lots of facts but don't have the context that the class provides. Without that context they will probably not pass a different set of questions. Exam results are thus poor indicators of potential in the real world.

Thus many people grow up in an environment that judges them on the numbers (how many exams, of what grade) in narrow subject areas. Then they get to work and it seems to be the same game. Everyone is judged in the context of their department on how much money, how much output, how many defects, how many complaints and so on. They're not assessed on 'how predictable is this operation?', or 'what are the underlying factors that influenced the score?', or 'what was the department's contribution to the whole organisation's performance?' or 'are people sharing their knowledge with colleagues?'

The Four-Student Model leads to these questions to keep in mind (as Pasteur observed) as you move about the workplace:

- What are people doing, and are they following an explicit process?
- What are the outcomes like if the process is followed/not followed?

Assessment approach
Our experience is that the great majority of the people you encounter, whether they work in your department or elsewhere, would really like things to work well and would be happy to join in with efforts to improve it. Time and time again we have encountered people who are entitled to be sceptical, based upon past experience, but who want to contribute. We believe you should assume that people started with this positive motivation even if they look cynical now, and that this should colour

---

1   This is a big topic of course, and illustrative of the overlap of our theme of process management with wider society. Because the task of examinations is on the whole to categorise people for further education or employment the results on their own are not indicative of how students studied. Hence the process of educating students is heavily distorted by efforts to ensure they get the best grades. As process managers we are subject to similar pressures – to get the results demanded – but we can illuminate our prospects for improvement by asking 'by what methods were the results obtained?' Once we have this information, and unlike the teachers, we are able to work to make changes to our part of the system, and those other parts that impact us.

your interpretation of what you see. If you demonstrate a willingness to learn, they may be more forthcoming than seemed likely at first.

As you move around your department, bear in mind one of the aspects of system thinking: understanding connections and interdependencies. Every component of your organisational system is connected in some way to the others. But cause and effect are often separated both in time and space, and this can lead to hidden sequences that people are unaware of, and thus may not be able to describe to you. As an outsider you can and must ask the questions that occur to you about why things vary, and keep on going beyond the obvious.

Find shortcuts to observe many people in everyday activities
Attend routine meetings, conference calls and so on. Watch, listen, experience, then have some discussion. Try to limit your questions at this stage to clarification rather than inviting justification.

How well is the central part of your function working?
The core activities that produce outputs for the benefit of the customer are often called the *Gemba*, which translates as the 'real place', and can be a useful term to use. It is that part of the organisation where the added value work is going on, and which thus determines its effectiveness and reputation. Watch and listen to what is happening. Not for just a few minutes, but maybe hours. Experience a shift changeover. If there is a suitable job to be done, do it. Warehouse handling, answering calls, clearing tables: anything to both experience the work and to demonstrate your interest and readiness to get your hands dirty. There are TV programmes that feature top executives adopting disguises to work on their shop floor to see what is happening, but in our experience that is completely wrong. It should always be a visible part of a top manager's job to witness the real work. Having practised it ourselves, we never found employees holding back on what they said. Far from it; they welcomed the opportunity to speak out, though as with everything else we can only have heard a partial story.

What do people think they are trying to accomplish?
Find out what they think is the purpose of the department / function you are observing. What are they trying to accomplish? We will return to this question later.

What data do people use?

Find out what information people collect, and what happens to it. What information do they get, and what do they do with it? How good is it all? How do they feel about it all? What information is visible at the workplace? How is it used?

Can people tell the difference between a problem and an abnormality in the work?

This is a more sophisticated question than it appears. In the overwhelming majority of cases people treat problems as if they were something special, when in fact they happen all the time. Each problem may get lots of attention – which may be necessary in order to placate the customer – but this attention tends to lead to fixes which undermine the normal running of the process. But if the problems are the result of regular operations they should be studied in the context of the continuing work, not in isolation.

However, an abnormality – something that is truly exceptional – is a learning and improvement opportunity even if it does not cause a problem. It indicates a shift from the regular performance, which might increase if not identified and rectified. We will discuss later how to recognise an abnormality and how to respond when you find one, but for now it can be helpful to see if anyone recognises the difference.

Anyone who has received good Statistical Process Control (SPC) training should be able to explain this readily.

What are the skills and competences?

Find out about what workplace training people have had, what cover there is for sickness, holidays, etc. to ensure consistency. How do people learn what they need to know? Is it just by working alongside colleagues or is there a specific curriculum? If people learn by watching or listening to colleagues the result may be an ever-increasing divergence from the original intention and policies.

What is IT's contribution?

You will need to figure out the role of IT resources, what they do as opposed to what they claim to do. How did it get to be that way? Who is the key person to liaise with; is there an ally?

How is work and organisational development managed?

If you work in a large organisation you need to discover, if you have not done so already, who is the owner of the processes you encounter in your department. A process owner is the person ultimately accountable for the overall process performance, to ensure it is capable of meeting its purpose. They have the authority to permit changes to it, and thus you will need to work with that person. However, just because there is a process owner identified it does not mean that the role is being properly fulfilled; this needs to be part of your discovery. But they certainly should not be kept in the dark! If there is no process owner the lines of authority for making changes may be obscure and you will need to find out what they may be.

Make sure you repeatedly clarify the reasons that you are doing all this – to learn, not to judge.

Keep a live diary, as much about impressions as specific items. But do note down anything which seems so obviously wrong and easy to change that you can't understand why it is like that. Keep these to yourself; we will return to making apparently obvious improvements in the next chapter. Some changes that look obvious and easy may have adverse consequences, and you should make your first decisions after reflection.

If you are not new in your role but would still like to revisit your workplace in this style, then there is no reason why you should not do so. However, people will interact with you based upon what they think of you, and you will see matters through the filter of your previous knowledge. You may jump to conclusions, explain things away and be insufficiently open-minded. You will not be able to ask the naive questions that a newcomer does. An external or new person sees different things to the residents. Some companies encourage cross-divisional assessment, and this can be powerful for all parties. In other cases you may wish to employ an external consultancy, and should expect a rapid and dispassionate summary. We explore this topic in Chapter 10.

Study the peripheral parts of your system

These include customers, suppliers, perhaps regulators, government bodies, consultants and training providers, trading partners, joint ventures and so on. All of these people have potential for insight. Each has different relationship with your part of the organisation, but our experience is that, if approached on a personal level, they will more than likely be delighted to help. If you assume that they would like your processes to work better, and ask for their help in doing that – without obligation at this stage – they will most likely say yes.

Be ready for long stories; you may be the first to take this enquiring approach. Use the four-student approach here, and take diligent notes.

In particular, build a picture of the customer experience. We will develop a model of categorising customer satisfaction in the next chapter, but meanwhile get close enough to some of them to sense the degrees of enthusiasm, commitment, resentment, etc. that are present. Make sure you have a good first-hand exposure and treat surveys with considerable caution. You may yourself have filled in survey forms – it's an enlightening thing to do – and should be well aware that they tell a very partial story depending on their purpose and how they were conducted. If you can find some customers who are considered to be troublemakers or a bit obsessed, then go and see them; one vocal complainer can be more worth listening to than a dozen satisfied customers. Anyone who complains a lot probably uses the product or service a lot and clearly cares about it if they are registering their point of view.

If you are in the retail field look carefully at the files that may have been passed to your PR office. How did things get so bad that a customer was driven to making that degree of effort in order to complain? How is it that the PR people can perhaps get things done that your function would not or could not organise? Are there targets or bonuses that conflict with providing customer satisfaction?

Build a map of your part of the organisation in relation to the wider system
Part of the task in the first study is to identify the components of the system in order that you can figure out how well they collaborate in order to achieve the aim. Use the template overleaf to make notes and bring your observations together. You will find that others will be interested in this approach as you use it, so much more helpful than a list for showing relationships and gaps.

This model is based upon that used by Dr W Edwards Deming from 1950 onwards. The system map does not replace the organisation diagram; clearly it's important for people to know who their boss is. But the organisation diagram does not show how the work flows or the relationships between processes, and it does not include customers, suppliers and others, who are part of the system whether paid as employees or not.

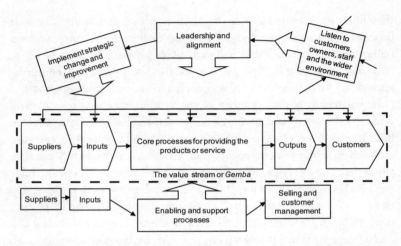

Around your part of the system, where does the variation come from?

On principle, consistency of outputs is generally a good thing: customers like predictability. However, it is hard to maintain and you should recognise that variation comes from everywhere. It is as likely to be as magnified as it is ameliorated in your part of the organisation, and variation in your outputs will be causing your customers many problems. It is hence always valuable to take steps that minimise variation, even if it is not clear why at first.

Some degree of variation is inherent in human organisations. Nothing repeats exactly, and all processes have a tendency to become increasingly disordered unless managed otherwise. For instance, people forget their training, machines wear, suppliers change their products, customer expectations move on. Keep on doing what you have always done and this tendency to disorder (known as entropy) will keep on generating ever more variable outputs. A manager's task must therefore not be limited to administrating, trying to keep things the same; they must be leaders of continual change just in order to avoid deterioration. This is a big subject, and we hope you will be interested enough to study it further. But for this book, you only need to accept a couple of assertions:

- The outputs of all processes vary, and you need to know how much variation is tolerable to your customers.
- It is useful to distinguish between variation that's part of the regular operations and which in itself can't tell us much (common cause), and variation which is surprising (assignable cause), and hence worth noting from the point of view of guiding your decisions.

We will expand on these two assertions in Chapters 3 and 4. For the moment let's consider where the variation comes from. A manufacturing version of the table below was proposed by one of the early Japanese experts, Dr Genichi Taguchi, in the early 1960s, and we at PMI added the service component in the late 1980s. The proportions are of course approximate, but they have been endorsed by thousands over those decades – people who come to recognise that variation reduction demands attention to more than just controlling their own everyday processes.

So where does the variation come from?

In manufacturing	In service environments
40% design of product and process	40% design of service and process
30% control of process	30% control of process
30% suppliers	30% customers

Another way of thinking about sources and consequences of variation is to construct a simple diagram to put it into context.

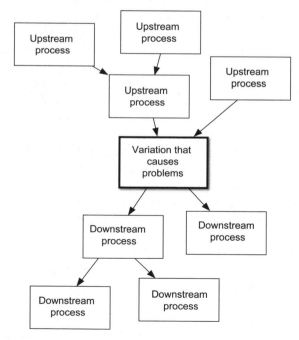

Variation context diagram

Therefore if you study only the current operation of your department you can only hope to impact about thirty per cent of the variation experienced by your customers. This is well worth debating with your boss as well as the suppliers. You can hope to make some rapid impacts on how *your* work works, but they may well not be enough. If they are not enough you will need wider ranging changes to make the differences your customers will notice, and that means going upstream to design and suppliers. We visit this issue in Chapter 8. Meanwhile, your study needs to uncover prospects for change within your function, so that you can learn and apply within your immediate authority at first.

Around your part of the system, what kinds of waste can you identify?
Practitioners have found it helpful to think about eight different categories of waste to watch out for. Clearly there are some overlaps and gaps, but if you have these in mind you will find plenty of candidates for attention.

1. **Defects**, which can include missing information, missed deadlines, perhaps incorrect versions or issue numbers of documents.
2. **Overproduction**, such as producing before the output is needed or can be used, thus needing space for storage and maybe finding that requirements have changed. Sometimes people produce more than has been asked for, perhaps just in case of potential problems or perhaps because they can't actually control the output accurately. We have also seen work being done on non-priority items ahead of more important things, possibly because it is easier.
3. **Waiting,** or delays between process steps. This can be hard to see, but it is common for waiting time to be much longer than the time spent actually working on the work; many administrative processes are dominated by waiting.
4. **Underutilised talents**, especially of process operators being treated like robots, their opinions and engagement not being sought, their experience not recognised.
5. **Transportation waste** is everywhere. Walking with documents, and walking to look for parts on an assembly operation are both commonplace. Look for flows to be in straight lines, not zigzags and loops.
6. **Inventory waste** is linked to waiting and perhaps overproduction. Look for piles of paper, queues of callers (or passengers at an

airport), work in progress in a manufacturing plant. Inventory is generated by processes that have not had enough thought about getting the pace of the operations aligned with customer demand.

7. **Motion** is waste resulting from poor design of the workplace. Whether the operation is manufacturing or service it should be laid out to enable the person to complete it with minimum personal effort.

8. **Excessive processing** is to be found everywhere – for instance, too many approvals for expenses, too many reviews for an advertisement. This is often the result of some distant problem which was 'fixed' by an extra process step but may even be completely irrelevant now. Look for the value to the customer and encourage people to report this kind of waste. Being new into your job will make it safe for them.

Waste is usually invisible to those surrounded by it. They may have noticed it when they started but, having got no response when asking 'why', it is now just how the work is done. Get into the habit of using this list in discussions, and be sure to respond later if you have decided nothing can be done for the moment. You are looking to reduce people's threshold of tolerance for waste, and they need to be rewarded by seeing change happen.

Waste and variation interact, always increasing trouble and never reducing it except by rare good fortune.

Waste is a good subject for attention in process management reviews and quality circles, as discussed later in Chapter 6.

How ready are people for a change in the way the work works?

Your exploration is likely to expose a lot of dissatisfaction. Most people will be aware of things not working so well, but have become resigned to it: this is human nature. If they have been putting up with it for a while – or perhaps there have been some change initiatives already that have faded – then they will unburden themselves to any new pair of ears.

However, this may not mean that they personally are ready to change, especially if it involves them taking personal risk, effort or adopting new behaviours. They may think they have tried before. They are also entitled to be sceptical about your commitment and longevity – think about Ann's sweepstake envelope. Being frustrated and blaming others becomes a way of getting through life and countless historic examples demonstrate it, from restrictive trade union practices to smoking and drinking, or even political beliefs. People may be aware of the consequences of not changing but not accept that it applies to them, and will not take the personal steps to move on.

Factors to be addressed in increasing readiness to change

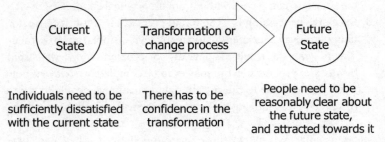

Individuals need to be sufficiently dissatisfied with the current state	There has to be confidence in the transformation	People need to be reasonably clear about the future state, and attracted towards it

Having sufficient dissatisfaction with how things are is one of the three components you will need to mobilise in order to get change on the way. You need to carefully consider the context in which dissatisfaction is expressed. If it seems to be in an environment of complacency, you will need to find ways to confront it, to get people to reflect on the unacceptability of carrying on like this, and put on the pressure as part of your role. However, if it's in an environment of threat and uncertainty, then a confrontational approach is likely to drive people into defensiveness. More effective in this case is for you to be supportive, protective and inspire people with a believable vision.

In either case you will need to articulate how things could be if they work properly, and that's the second of the components: a vision. It has to be both attractive and clear, regardless of how ambitious you may be. If there is no defined aim there cannot be a system for improvement. We will address this in Chapter 2.

Recording your findings

> A hidden connection is stronger than an obvious one.
> **Heraclitus, c500 BCE**

You will have gathered a great deal of information, some easily, but much rather hidden, particularly that which is cross-functional, and that could have the most value. You need to capture it, as suggested earlier, and then to make sense of it, relating and prioritising it to guide your decisions. You need to start at the high level, across your department, before later agreeing with your people a process to work on.

Summarise the process in its context

Construct a rough diagram to summarise the key components of your part of the system. Under each of the categories list the details such as organisations, people, measures, targets. Note sources of variation and problems. Details of a SIPOC diagram can be found in PMI's handbook *The Process Manager.*

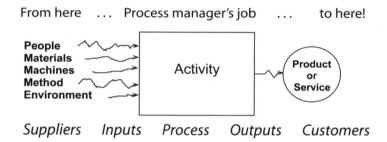

If you encounter any trained process improvement staff, or Six Sigma or Lean qualified people, they should readily take to this approach and be able to help you formalise and develop it.

Map the process flow

Even if you are not familiar with process mapping, do try to represent your understanding of the work you have been learning about by using some sort of flow diagram. Representing work steps by boxes, the flow of goods, information or services as arrows, and the decisions and feedback as loops is far more effective than making lists. A flowchart enables you to record questions, observations, concerns and so on next to the point at which they seem to emerge, and in turn this will grow in value as you lead further investigation and improvement.

You could do this mapping work with others in the department, which helps their learning too, of course. And it also provides a good basis for your note taking when quickly travelling round on your first visit,.

You will also find guidance on process mapping in *The Process Manager*, and in online and classroom training.

Reflect on the maturity of what you have discovered

After a few days or weeks you will come to the close of your initial investigations. In fact, in spite of your efforts to stay clear of the everyday pressures whilst you learn, urgent issues have no doubt intruded to some extent from quite early on. You have been carrying out an assessment, and now is the time to summarise what you have found. You may have some experience as an assessor, in which case you will have recognised many parallels but no doubt reflected on some omissions in our approach. These relate to your purpose; you are looking to learn, not to assign a score.

As the new (or old) boss your primary motivation needs to be as a learner and helper and not as a judge, as must be the case with a third-party assessor. In Chapter 2 we explore the parallels of our approach with that of a medical doctor seeking to diagnose a patient's condition in order to work together to improve it. That is far from the feelings generated by quality assessments where the dominating sense of those being assessed is 'how do we need to come across in order to win a prize?'. In spite of the differences with a quality prize assessment there are some useful aspects of that process that can be adopted.

Process maturity matrix

The table below provides a quick reference and a basis for reflection later. You will no doubt find that you can put both positive and negative comments against every level. However, the overriding question – 'is the work delivering to its customer-based goals?' – is not in the matrix. No amount of apparently impressive process management boxes ticked can substitute for effective management of the work that the processes enable. Doing the wrong things in a prizewinning way is not what work should be about.

Level	Meaning	Comments at time of first study
1	The key processes are identified.	
2	Ownership of them has been established, and their purpose is understood.	
3	They are formally flowcharted / documented and standardised operations can be seen.	
4	Appropriate and visible measures are used to monitor the processes and enable learning.	
5	Feedback from customers, suppliers and other processes is sought and used as the basis for improvement.	
6	An improvement and review mechanism is in place with targets for improvement.	
7	Processes are systematically managed for continual improvement, and learning is shared.	
8	The processes are benchmarked against best practice.	
9	The processes are regularly challenged and re-engineered if required.	
10	The processes are a role model for other organisations.	

In addition, the matrix highlights the foundations which must be laid before more sophisticated ideas can be useful. No amount of measuring, reviewing, benchmarking, etc. can mitigate the lack of basic understanding and discipline in process definition and adherence.

Assessing a whole system: the dream of the Four Es

The success of those remarkable organisations that have worked to optimise their whole system over many decades can be summed up under four headings, each beginning with the letter E.

The organisation is achieving its goals, and can demonstrate its management and improvement approach...

- **Everywhere.** Across the whole organisation, including strategy development, everyday work and projects.
- **Every day.** Leaders understand and can explain the relationship between how they approach their work and the overall improved results they have achieved.
- By **Everyone.** The approach is used in depth where appropriate and can be explained by line managers and staff routinely, not just the improvement personnel.
- For **Ever.** It has clearly been applied and developed over many years.

If you visit leading organisations across Asia – such as Tata, Samsung, Toyota, Hyundai and Thai Ceramics – you will find these characteristics readily explained by staff ranging from the CEO to production supervisors. The approach really is their way of working, integrated with their most strategic goals and operating culture. There are of course many successful western-owned corporations, but few with such explicit in-depth emphasis on their work processes as well as innovation.

Although the Four Es might seem a very ambitious series of statements, you can make great progress towards them in your department. The case to be built in Chapter 2 – 'what should be happening?' – will be taking the first steps towards them, and we will revisit the subject in Chapter 9.

How ready are *you* to change how you work?

The 'readiness to change' structure introduced earlier is useful in developing your own behaviour as time goes on. You will have found plenty of information that leads you to believe that 'we can't go on like this anymore', and as the leader you will constantly have to think hard about your own readiness to change, and work on it.

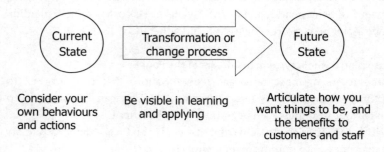

Current State → Transformation or change process → Future State

Consider your own behaviours and actions

Be visible in learning and applying

Articulate how you want things to be, and the benefits to customers and staff

Ann's reflections

Ann pondered her conclusions in terms of the System of Profound Knowledge. Most of her notes related to more than one of the parts and this was initially frustrating. However, she came to appreciate that although she was not sure exactly how to categorise issues, at least she was covering each of the four components and how they interacted.

She had made a first attempt at drawing the department in the format of a system map, and had shared this with some of her people.

Ann's rough map of her department as a system

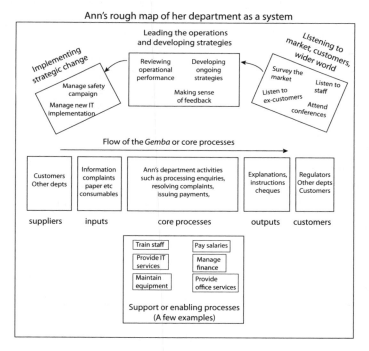

Systems thinking:

● People didn't seem to understand their role within the organisation as a system.

● Most people thought the aim within the system was about targets for keeping down the cost of complaints.

● There was little process language, such as flow, waste, feedback; it was dominated by incidents, numbers.

● The little improvement activity that she had been shown was not integrated within a programme.

- People reacted to the varieties of customer needs with irritation and frustration, especially with language difficulties.
- The various functions that should have been providing support – finance, HR, health and safety and so on – seemed more intent on their own agendas than helping her to serve customers better.

Variation:

- Performance of the processes was very variable; some days were better than others, but she had little idea why. Workplace organisation wasn't very consistent; she had various pictures to show that.
- Customers and suppliers regarded the organisation with toleration rather than enthusiasm, and were especially frustrated with inconsistencies.
- People were not even thinking about the standardisation of their work through formalised processes.
- Waste was everywhere, and was not remarked upon unless extreme.
- Few people had any idea about how to interpret and react appropriately to variation.

Theory of knowledge:

- Nobody had heard of the Plan Do Study Act Cycle.
- Words were often misused and there was a lot of confusion, even on basic terms like process time.
- There was some appetite for learning about their organisation and how it worked, but it was variable.

Psychology:

- There was not much warmth in the atmosphere when the boss arrived in the room.
- By and large, people thought it risky to volunteer or take responsibility for improving the organisation; it was someone else's job.
- There was quite a lot of cynicism on the surface about their work experiences.
- Most people felt they were not well informed about the business.
- But salaries seemed OK – and people had affection for the firm, though she was not clear why.
- With all this, she thought, there was plenty of scope, and she was definitely unhappy enough to be ready to try some new things. However, she knew she had first to explore how things should be, before moving rapidly to test some ways of getting there.

2 What should be happening?

Without ambition one starts nothing. Without work one finishes nothing. The prize will not be sent to you. You have to win it.
Ralph Waldo Emerson, US writer, 1803–82

Ann's story

Tomorrow morning, first thing, Ann would be meeting with her boss again. She made her final notes. Two days later there would be the postponed planning meeting, but tomorrow's was to share her findings and get agreement for her ideas on the initial improvement work. She would need support from her boss later in some of the politics around the company but, initially at least, she felt that some worthwhile changes could be tried within the department.

The impressions she had made during her visits and conversations around the function had been mixed. The work was getting done but people seemed to be working long hours, and some of the customers had dispiriting tales to tell in spite of apparently satisfactory survey ratings. There was resentment towards a recent IT installation, but overall people felt the company deserved its reputation as a reliable and conscientious supplier. She wasn't sure they were ready to make the kind of changes she thought were needed. She was intending to speak to the consultants who worked on this scheme to see what they thought.

She had identified a couple of serious issues that needed to be dealt with, although no one was clear how they could be settled easily, and there were some trivial policy irritations that should be rapidly resolved. She had prepared her boss to be ready to hear about ideas for setting up a team to develop plans and test some solutions, and hoped to come out of the meeting with support. She needed to be sure he would back some rapid tests and to ask a couple of her colleagues to provide some team members. She wanted him to be patient, allowing the team to properly research the various possibilities, and not feel pressured to jump to conclusions as seemed to be his nature. She also wanted to understand his long-term ambitions for the function; people had expressed some confusion about where things were going.

Developing meaningful goals: generating theories

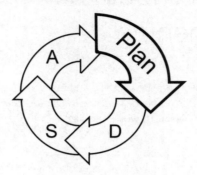

However long you take to explore and enquire into current operations and their prospects, you will encounter a mass of impressions and data, and explanations for them. Some will seem logical, perhaps even common sense, and there may indeed be some obvious decisions to make. However, much of what you have seen and heard will be confused and contradictory, and opinions about urgency might apparently clash with those about importance.

> You have to be burning with 'an idea, or a problem, or a wrong that you want to right.' If you're not passionate enough from the start, you'll never stick it out.
> **Steve Jobs, entrepreneur and CEO of Apple, 2010**

> If one does not know to which port one is sailing, no wind is favourable.
> **Seneca, c.4 BCE–65 CE**

Two thousand years between these thoughts – having the right goals is evidently important. Before you make initial conclusions about actions you need to think hard about the end that everyone is going to need to bear in mind. Then you can attempt a diagnosis of why it's not already being achieved.

This Three-Question Model, developed by Tom Nolan, Lloyd Provost, Ron Moen and colleagues, provides a simple reference point throughout your improvement efforts.

What are you trying to accomplish?

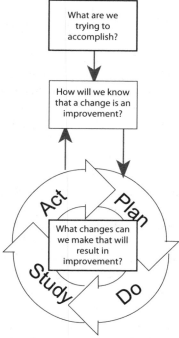

This first question is relevant at every scale, from a meeting through to a top management group considering the long term. In many cases you will find that some people have not shared their thoughts about it; it's just yet another meeting to get through. When we introduce this question to management teams it usually turns out that people have assumed that they know the answer but actually have contradictory goals in mind. When they have to refer to a printed card you know there's something wrong. Some are focussed on the customer, others on costs, others on safety, for instance. It's hardly surprising that they disagree on priorities when it comes to making decisions.

Let's consider first some of the primary goals for a process, and then some ancillary ones. You will need to balance your ambitions across them. You may also find some contradiction between the external goals – derived from the customer, the environment and so on – and internal or political goals from managers. You may have to make a compromise with the internal ones in order to progress with the 'real' ones.

What are the customer goals?

Ultimately the customers are the arbiters of the life or death of your organisation. If they choose others, or simply refuse to engage with you if they find they have no choice, the organisation will eventually cease to function.

This can take a long time to show up, as with much of the western-owned motor industry through the 1960s, 70s and 80s. Customers slowly drifted towards Japanese makes in order to find reliability, cost and features that were not being provided by home manufacturers. The home manufacturers misunderstood these reasons, blaming their workers or the exchange rates or appealing to patriotism. Their profits cycled between boom and bust whilst their Japanese rivals built up cash mountains and global production facilities. The home producers ran campaigns to persuade buyers to act on patriotic instincts or lobbied governments to protect them, but the tide of better, more reliable and cheaper imported cars eventually swamped them. Rather too late, many companies tried to adopt the principles and tools developed in Japan, and those that succeeded in doing this are those thriving today. Customers have done well, but many people lost their jobs along the way and investors had poor returns much of the time.

There can sometimes seem to be rather a lot of process management illustrations from the global motor industry, and the applications can seem distant to a school, hospital or call centre. However, we have all witnessed and benefitted from the transformations in the motor industry and the leadership and organisational principles are universal. We can all learn a lot from a global industry that has been learning about optimising itself for sixty years.

One of the key principles is the emphasis on customer satisfaction and delight, pursued over many decades. This has underpinned the financial success and employee satisfaction that can be seen today in the best Japanese-owned companies. None are perfect and little can be copied directly, but even their problem resolution methods have useful lessons for all of us.

The Kano Model

So, from the very first these companies have focussed on their customers – how to understand them, satisfy and then delight them. Customers have many ways of reacting to the products or services they experience.

The model shown below, developed many years ago by Dr Noriaki Kano, provides a very useful way of thinking about what you provide to your customers, and you can use it to categorise your findings so far. It helps find some goals that, if you meet them, customers will notice and appreciate.

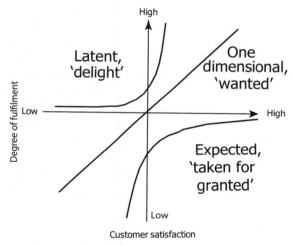

The model has three categories:

Expected. 'Expected' factors, shown in the bottom right corner, are those the customer assumes will be present without having to ask for them, probably without thinking. As such, they are hardly noticed when they are provided but are a cause of significant annoyance if they are missing. The opportunity thus exists to explore people's dissatisfaction with this focus – what they might be annoyed about but don't describe. You may have to observe them using your outputs. What do they complain about amongst themselves? What bad experiences have they had? What do you notice that's wrong but which they don't seem to notice? These investigations often yield a spectrum of information that would normally remain hidden.

Poor performance in the 'expected' category is thus generally identifiable by watching or listening to customers without prompts. Information resulting from asking questions is in the 'wanted' category.

Wanted. We derive 'wanted' criteria from two main sources: being exposed to information that attracts us, or alternatively experiences from our past that we wish to repeat or avoid. There is a simple way to discover these criteria: ask the customer. In particular, it is worth identifying customers who push your product or service to extremes and asking them. You may well find that people who test you to the limit are the best source of information, particularly if they are long-term enthusiasts. Bear in mind the difference between frequent users and demanding users. If you were trying to improve a word-processing software package you would get one view from junior secretarial staff, but they might be unlikely to expose opportunities for innovation. But if you listen to people trying to use the software to prepare leaflets or posters (perhaps they do not have access to specialist packages), you will see the limitations more clearly and perhaps be able to address them and broaden the appeal of your product.

This search for extreme users is particularly valid with internal customers. Many of these are possibly routinely satisfied or tolerant, but some may have strong views as a result of having to do workarounds or something non-standard when things change just a little. We do recognise that the dissatisfied and demanding user can be tough to engage with, but their ideas can be well worth the effort.

For an illustration of this we remember a delivery issue with some very large aerospace components. Because these were made in the US but used in the UK, the customer and supplier were thoroughly separated and did not understand each other's facilities. When the suppliers visited the customer they were surprised to find that they turned each large piece over – which required a special crane – before using it. A very short discussion revealed that no one had thought to ask if these pieces could be despatched the other way up. Once the question was posed, the change was easily made. This cost nothing to the supplier and meant a considerable saving for the customer: all down to observation and discussion.

You may get some idea of 'wants' from a survey, but don't rely on these to be complete. The answers will be sterile in comparison with experiencing what the customers experience, and asking them on the spot what they think. All of your staff who interact with customers are potential discoverers of customer 'wants', as well as being obvious listening posts for complaints. They may well see your product or service being used for something it was never deigned for, and you could be the first to commercialise this if you hear about it.

Delight. The 'delight' factors are at a different level. By definition the customer does not know what they are until they materialise. Their potential may be identified if suppliers develop their understanding of the customer experience and exceed the expressed wants of their customers in a way that they had not expected. Sometimes suppliers can determine delight factors by analysing carefully what the customers do and what they talk about and interpreting this into a new offer. Many successful organisations owe their competitive edge to their ability to generate these delight factors, repeatedly keeping themselves ahead of others by using their specialist knowledge to provide something not previously even thought of. In fact, unless you can keep ahead of what customers say they want, you will be reduced to the level of a commodity supplier, only responding to specifications that are open to everyone. This innovation must be to suit a customer need or want, however; people might not pay for clever technology for its own sake.

Innovation tends to become self-perpetuating if you keep your eyes open. For instance, when Apple first put a movie camera in the iPad they did not expect it to become a major feature. But now that people are using the iPad routinely as a movie camera, Apple have been adding refinements to take advantage and encourage its further adoption.

In order to delight people you may consider an alternative to an old cliché: 'treat others as you would be treated yourself'. A customer-focussed person will 'treat others as *they* would like to be treated'. Much more powerful, but not necessarily easy, for it implies discovery and empathy – others may not be like you.

A curious feature of this top left part of the Kano diagram is that a new service or product feature does not necessarily have to be perfect when first released in order to generate delight. We remember text messaging, for instance. In the first year or so after its provision the telephone companies that provided it won many customers from those that did not. Yet a couple of years later the early performance levels had been completely overtaken; it turned out that the launch service wasn't really very good. The company that launched with a just OK product that worked prevailed over the companies that were waiting until the development was perfected.

Today, of course, texting is a 'must have' feature, one taken for granted. In general the features you provide to your customers drift from top left to bottom right of the diagram, becoming commodities all too quickly.

Your long-term survival depends on continually finding things that will delight your customers, allowing yesterday's innovation to become today's 'must have'.

In summary, at this stage you may find that your organisation is not doing well in some aspects of 'must-have quality'. If this is the case, such aspects should take a high priority for change. Then you can progress to 'wanted' or 'delight' factors. Customers will not be impressed with clever new features if they are being let down on the basics.

What are the financial goals – the voice of the owners?

Customer demand provides the energy for your organisation, but money is its life blood, no matter whether you run a commercial business or a not for profit. You must be clear about what the financial goals are, who cares about them and how they like to be communicated with. In a big organisation the obvious people are your boss and the financial director. But you may find that your colleagues have a strong opinion too; perhaps your function has been running over budget and their spending is being held back as a consequence. Or maybe your division's success has been subsidising some poor performers.

In a smaller organisation financial performance will have a direct effect on all your surrounding stakeholders. You need sufficient income to cover costs and sufficient cash to reduce any overdrafts. There is no getting away from the need to rapidly become familiar with the credit taken by customers or allowed by suppliers, and the conditions and costs associated with that credit or debt. Your organisation has to provide for pension and tax payments, and to have a surplus left at the end. This may be for distribution to shareholders, investment in new facilities or just to build up a cushion against future perils.

Being a process-oriented manager does not – indeed, cannot – change these financial imperatives. Your early investigations will probably have exposed many arbitrary and contradictory targets that may need to be challenged and perhaps changed. But cash in the bank is not arbitrary; it is the seed corn for your future, whether you're in a commercial or a not-for-profit organisation, and eventually you will need to be clear on how your work interacts with this number. Money is thus another criteria for prioritising early improvement tests.

This is, of course, a huge subject and must not be trivialised. Arrange to get some training in accounting for non-finance managers in order to better understand the concepts and language you will encounter. But don't just listen and accept what is taught. The experiences of the last few years entitle you to challenge concepts you don't understand, especially if they seem to run counter to the overall goal of delighting customers as the only route to future prosperity. Surviving the next year in cash terms is important right now, but it must not be allowed to override development and innovation for the future. And anyone who advocates rewarding managers for hitting financial targets has clearly not studied the evidence.

Other goals

Many other goals will become evident during your studies. Some are known about and discussed, but there are likely to be others that you may have spotted but other people have not. Though they need to be achieved, they may not even have been measured yet. Some examples, in no particular order, include:

- Pollution
- Safety
- Equal opportunities
- Fair trade
- Carbon emissions
- Employee skills
- Reputation in society

These are each big subjects in themselves with books, training and conferences to inform practitioners. However, the performance in every one of these arenas is the result of processes at work. The variation in your department's achievement of whatever demands are made is the result of variation in the design, inputs and operation of your processes. The methodology to improve any of them should be based upon the PDSA Cycle, as described in Chapter 3.

How will you know if a change is improvement?

This second question of the Three-Question Model follows naturally from defining goals. Every process has a variety of characteristics that indicate its output performance which are called results measures. Some will be critical, but there are always others that are important too. In every case you will need to satisfy yourself that sufficient measures are known that are practical to collect and mean something useful. This is sometimes not as easy as it may appear at first sight.

Consider a pizza. The diner's initial judgement will be based upon some relatively easy to measure features such as size, colour and amount of topping. However, their memory of how pleased they are will be dominated by taste, smell and texture, perhaps the stringiness of the cheese – all much harder to quantify. You can design in some control of some of these measurable factors, but may have to accept that the chef's value judgement on the day could be more important than, say, a specific diameter or the weight of the dough.

Thus, a task at this early stage in learning about the work is to define some results measures for each aspect of the process which is considered important. It would be an advantage to talk with some old hands within the organisation and with some customers, but be prepared to have to modify these views later in the light of experience. Different customers may have contrasting views, and it may take a lot of evidence to build up some patterns and standardise the numbers that will be used. It's quite possible that different patterns will demand quite different approaches. Consider a restaurant providing meals before curtain up at the theatre. Time is a dominant factor; customers will not come back if they are delayed. But an hour later the diners might be romantic couples, and they might value a lengthy interval between courses. If you wish to serve both markets all the staff need to be aware of which they are dealing with, especially if an early couple is not going to a theatre, or a late pair wants a quick bite before the next train. None of them will appreciate being interrupted in deep conversation just to be asked whether everything is OK so you have some data to look at on your spreadsheet!

In summary, results measures are necessary for judging the success of your work. It is also fruitful to clarify results measures for your suppliers' outputs because they may not know which need to be controlled on your behalf. However, results measures are often not very useful for monitoring your work as it happens, as they only emerge at the end of the process and may also be destructive, as in tests of materials such as metals or holidays (or even cake). Thus you will need to discover internal, or process, measures, that correlate with the results, but are generated as the work is done. We will explore these in Chapter 3. The pizza chef has many process measures, such as the amount of various ingredients, the speed and duration of mixing, the time, temperature and fan speed in the oven and so on.

You need to discover which results measures are most useful during the improvement tests, and then refine them by use in everyday operations. You will realise that targets need to be considered very carefully, and that the data must always be considered in the context of the process. You will also discover that in some cases success is not confirmed by a number but by a feeling, such as the ambience of a shop or the atmosphere in a call centre. Data are useful, but rarely tells the whole story.

You need to keep track of the overall process performance through several categories or dimensions:

- Effectiveness: how well the work works as seen by the customers and the outside world.
- Efficiency: how much resources are used. Effective processes tend to be efficient as they generate minimal scrap, rework and waste, but apparently efficient processes may not be at all effective.
- Adaptability: how well they can change as needed without losing effectiveness and efficiency. This one may demand generating variety of output, not to be confused with accidental variation of the process or its components.

Your ambition: 'on target with minimum variation'

This can become a universal rallying cry both for the whole organisation and for individual operations. When used with sensible results and process data, in the context of work processes, you will find it powerful. It can become part of the overall vision for your department.

For 'on target with minimum variation' to be useful it requires that the goals are relevant to the customer. There may also be some agreed criteria that would result in rejection or a claim if not met. This could be a time for a delivery, a dimension for a component, or perhaps a reliability target. When you get this right your assessment of the target and variability of the output will enable you to anticipate the customer response.

'On target with minimum variation' is not the same as complying with a specification: 'OK / not OK'. In this mindset anything that is apparently in specification is regarded as good, and the same as anything else that complies. Conversely, anything outside the specification is deemed a failure and all failures are equally bad.

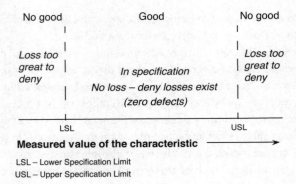

LSL – Lower Specification Limit
USL – Upper Specification Limit

This black and white attitude is often very unhelpful. From examinations at school to inspections of hospital wards or testing of goods delivered, forms are filled in, boxes ticked, claims made against failure. Immense effort is put into getting the right score regardless of what happens to individual customers, patients, etc. In turn this leads to the loss of valuable insight – because although everything varies, if the only information is pass or fail then there is not much to learn from. Time is spent investigating the few per cent that fail and not the vast majority of outputs from the same system, which also vary but conform – and so are not studied.

In addition, the problem can become exaggerated when results are averaged. Always keep the whole of the data, including its variation and not just pass / fail judgements or averages.

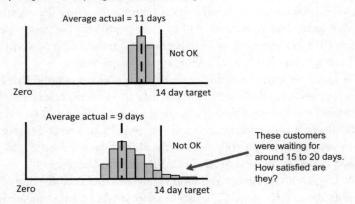

Unpredictable variation leads to costs to the rest of the system, whether they are evident within your part of it or not, and perhaps even if they seem to be within the specification. You will find in your investigations that many of your existing specifications are not based upon rigorous analysis and will benefit from extended study and redefinition at some stage.

Process capability and Six Sigma targets

There is a potential conflict here. We may desire to get the process on target with minimum variation, but the customer is entitled to require us to manage to their specification. We need some standard way of comparing our achievement to the wider world, in particular with competitors. This is called process capability, abbreviated to Cpk, and is closely related to the Six Sigma performance which readers may have heard of. This is a big topic, one too complex to do justice to here. If you are interested there are descriptions and training programmes available, but at this stage your basic understanding of processes and their improvement is much more important.

Cpk and Six Sigma relate the customer need or want – i.e. the specification – to the ability of the output of the process to be kept centred over an extended time on the target and within this specification, in spite of its variation.

In the manufacturing industry there are tens of thousands of processes across the world that routinely use this approach to reduce failure rates to less than two or three per million, hence the astonishing reliability of the cars, cameras and so on that are constructed in this way. Many such components can be assembled in complex products, without inspection, with the confidence that they will always work properly.

The degree of ambition in performance is for you to work out for your environment. If you have many processes that consist of interactions with

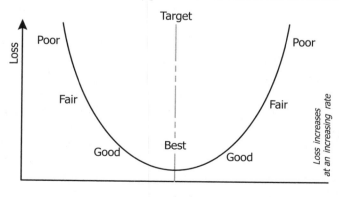

other people then failure rates of a few per cent may be a big improvement on historical performance. The concept of 'on target with minimum variation' is always valid, and leads to useful discussions.

The diagram on page 33 shows how the variation away from the target leads to increased costs downstream.

Diagnosing your part of the system

Much of what you do at this stage of your investigations has things in common with medical diagnosis.

When you visit a medical practitioner with an ailment they will follow a series of steps to diagnose what is going on in order to make some intervention and help you to get better:

1. They will observe your symptoms, measure various characteristics, ask for information, and so on. They will (should) seek information not just about the apparent immediate problem, but also – hopefully – about all of your person, and perhaps about your family and your home or work life and so on.
2. They will synthesise all of this information into an overview and compare your symptoms with what they know about 'well' people like you, and come to some initial judgement – theories – about why things are like they are. They should share this with you to see how much you agree.
3. They will then outline a prognosis to you: what is likely to happen if things carry on as they have been. This may well be quite depressing, but if you have understood how they came to that opinion, and bearing in mind what has happened so far, you should be ready to do some things differently.
4. The next step is for them to suggest that if certain changes are made or treatments undergone there will be a new prognosis – hopefully an improvement on what is likely if nothing changes. These changes may be as simple as taking some medication, but could well involve you in changes of diet or exercise, stopping smoking, drinking less and so on. In other words, it is rarely enough for the patient to be a neutral recipient of a treatment; their actions are likely to be fundamental to their recovery. As we all know, it is unlikely to be easy for a patient to make these changes and persist in them for years. Most people need ongoing support.

Hopefully you will see that your activities so far have been moving between 1 and 3 of these stages, working up to 4. You have been listening, watching, measuring, perhaps visiting other reputable organisations to see what success looks like, and talking with your people at every stage to see their reactions to your interpretation. Success at the next stage depends upon them agreeing with your dissatisfaction and being attracted by your ideas for how it could be – so that they will join with you on trying some improvements.

Part of their preparedness to change is likely to depend upon you demonstrating that you are ready to change yourself. This may not apply so much if you are new to the role, but may be critical if you have been the boss for a while and are thus looking to improve work that you are already identified with.

Getting buy-in to the diagnosis, and planning a trial

This is step four of the diagnosis. You need to be clear about what you think is worth doing and why, and ready to build the confidence of your key people to go along with it. Unlike a doctor, it is most unlikely that you will be able to propose a tested, reliable solution; it will have to be discovered and hence the need for careful trial. No one has been in quite the same position that you and your department are in, no one is trying to get to the same place and no one has trodden the path you are embarking on. This may seem a little intimidating but it is where the principles and methods come in. They have been developed over decades in similar circumstances, helping leaders to learn how to make the right plans to use the proven tools.

Current State	Transformation or change process	Future State
Individuals need to be sufficiently dissatisfied with the current state	There has to be confidence in the transformation	People need to be reasonably clear about the future state, and attracted towards it

You therefore need to find ways to get your managers, supervisors and staff involved with hearing about your initial conclusions, and jointly agreeing where to make a start. It will require a meeting, the first of many, to ensure you are all understanding the issues and agreeing to the actions.

Diagnosis and planning meeting

> Doubt is not a pleasant condition. But certainty is an absurd one.
> **Voltaire, French writer, 1694–1778**

This activity is about generating and sharing theories – explanations of cause and effect about the work – built on your first study and their prior knowledge. The theories must not be thought of as having to be 'right', but they do need to be made explicit at this stage so that a later study can use the data in the trials to see if they stand up to the real world.

The meeting should carefully follow sensible disciplines to help it work properly.

1. Before (Plan)
- Clarify the need with those attending.
- Circulate the objectives and agenda in advance.
- Make sure the arrangements for the room, refreshments etc. are organised.
- Get the roles and responsibilities agreed ahead of time.
- If there are any other key contributors, make sure they know what's expected of them.
- Think through possible barriers and provide for them (such as your boss calling for another meeting on that day).

2. During (Do)
- Keep to the agenda.
- Take any expectations and hopes from the attendees that may be in addition to the agenda items.
- Honour the timing contract and negotiate any changes with all the attendees.
- Practise and facilitate good meeting behaviour.
- Provide a 'car park' for new issues that haven't got time to be debated.

- Watch out for jargon.
- Identify clear next steps.

3. End of the meeting (Study)
- Review the next steps and ensure someone has agreed to take each one forward.
- Evaluate the effectiveness of the meeting in regard to objectives and expectations, and capture benefits and concerns.

4. After the meeting (Act)
- Circulate a summary including next steps, and do it promptly.
- Incorporate benefits and concerns into next meeting plan.
- Lead or facilitate the activities on the next steps.

Activities in this first meeting should include constructing a process map of your function. With this context in mind you have the best chance of selecting a part of your system that all would agree is causing enough problems to be worth the effort, whilst not being too ambitious to be dealt with in a few weeks.

In this meeting you should also ensure that everyone has one more chance to suggest immediate and obvious improvements or changes that don't require policy decisions. There are likely to be many candidates:

- Obvious duplication of effort.
- Collecting data that never gets used.
- Replacing broken furniture, damaged signs, perhaps doing some decorating – anything that is a result of lethargy or disinterest in the past and which people think influences the atmosphere.
- There could also be ideas about workplace organisation that you may want to try changing, but don't expect miracles. Such things are symptoms of other attitudes, as you may remember about your teenage bedroom!

The first meeting provides a vehicle for you to show how you intend things to be – following processes that help people see what is happening, and sharing learning so that they can be improved. There will be many other meetings, and each of them needs to follow this approach. You will refine them with practice and set the scene for activities, especially meetings, that you cannot see.

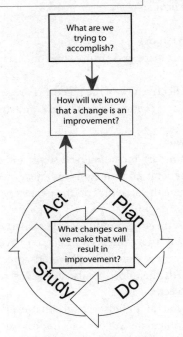

After a lot of thought, Ann had decided to use the Three-Question Model to summarise the goals of her job and how success would be judged. She had not been at all sure that such simple questions could produce useful answers, but in fact they had done. Furthermore, they had been very easy to explain to her boss and to colleagues – so easy that no one could understand why they hadn't been using them before.

- She would be seeking to support the reputation of the company by helping customers in their transactions.
- They would know if these changes were improvements by customer feedback and the number of complaints, especially those escalating beyond her function.
- They would have to discover the appropriate changes by repeated trials.

She made some notes against the System of Profound Knowledge headings again.

Systems thinking:
- Clarity and promptness would delight the customers in the current state of affairs, together with honesty when things went wrong.
- If her function was working well in optimising the organisation as a system, nobody would notice them. That could be a problem but she would tackle it when it appeared.
- The meeting had agreed there was scope for rapid improvement in one or two areas so she would get her boss's endorsement for this right away.
- She would need to approach sales, IT and HR for help in what they did for her, and maybe enrol them as active contributors to the improvement effort.

Variation:
- If processes were consistent and capable – in other words, effective – they would run faster and cost less.
- She wasn't very impressed by what she had seen and heard of the internal improvement people as far as knowledge of variation was concerned.

Theory of knowledge:
- There were too many pet theories about how things could be and not enough carefully considered ideas that could be tested.
- There was much room for improvement in how people defined what they meant: the same words could mean different things and different words the same thing.

Psychology:
- The meeting had gone well, really well; people had liked the structure, liked the idea that it would run to time and they had some good outcomes.
- When she had spoken to the consultant who had been working in her department a few months ago he told her that one of her managers was occasionally faking his data. She would watch this closely over the next months.

They were ready to get on with some trial changes, but for now she closed the book and went out to see how things were doing at the start of the next shift.

3 Trying out some changes

No task is a long one but the task on which one dare not start. It becomes a nightmare.
Baudelaire, French writer, 1821–67

Ann's story

Only one flip chart pen worked! Ann strode impatiently down the corridor to the admin office, trying to keep calm. She had left, so she thought, plenty of time to prepare for this meeting; had even visited the room the previous day to make sure. But someone had moved the tables around since then and there was nobody else here yet to help put them back. So she had done that and put her pre-prepared flipcharts on the stand, then discovered the age of the pens in the rack. Not the ideal way to start. But at least the conference phone was up and running and nobody had said they couldn't come.

She had settled with her boss on the two initial projects that arose out of the diagnosis meeting, and this was the launch meeting for the first one. She had found that her department was responsible for sending compensation cheques to customers who had suffered poor service. She had then been amazed and dismayed to discover that some of these cheques could apparently be sent to the customer with no explanation of what they were for and why they were for the amount stated. There were not many of these incidents – though nobody was quite sure how many – but some of them generated severe complaints, particularly when the customer complained again and couldn't get the problem corrected. Two months previously one had featured in a Sunday newspaper after a customer was unable to get an answer from the department.

Initially Ann had felt that this problem might be too big to resolve quickly, possibly crossing several functional responsibilities and needing IT time and spend to put it right. But in discussion with her own people, and her boss, it seemed that they might be able to put a temporary fix in place to protect the customers. Her boss had even agreed that he would fund some extra staff if they were needed in the short term. This would take some pressure off, and he did not want the CEO chasing him again from his conservatory on a Sunday morning! As Ann put the new pens on the flipchart stand she heard the first people coming along the corridor....

Testing theories: it's time to get started

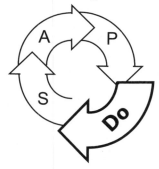

Yes, it's time to get on with *doing* something. Having got this far, you may think you have logic on your side. You have listened and watched, counted and reasoned. You have figured out some goals, worked out how you might monitor progress and selected one or two problems to focus upon. You have generated some agreement from your team and maybe some colleagues, and gained the support of your boss. The next job is to set up some trials. With all this preparation it should be pretty straightforward. It shouldn't be too hard to test some theories, pick the response that works best and move on, implementing it in the regular work...

Why projects fail

Not so fast. If improving things were that simple, there would be a lot more successful fixes, change projects and programmes. Unfortunately, logic and evidence, tools and methods are not enough. This graphic, which clients often refer to as the hamburger model, illustrates the fact that progress from the unsatisfactory present to the desired future has several interacting components.

After Jack Gibb

The tangible parts of a change – the tasks and the process – are unfortunately only part of the picture. Any number of factors can dominate thinking and behaviour to the exclusion of apparent logic: how people feel about what is going on, what they imagine might be coming or why it's like it is at the moment. You only have to watch a sport to see this. Highly competent players have bad days; middle-ranking athletes may have a run of exceptional form. Sometimes you wonder if it's the same tennis player in the second set that you were watching five minutes ago in the first one. That's part of the appeal of sport to a spectator, however frustrating it is when your team unaccountably fails to perform as it could. Just to complicate matters, we tend to see patterns in performance where there are none – reading significance into the natural variation that leads people to do better on some days than others for no particular reason at all.

Or consider politics and religion, where people's beliefs may (only may!) influence how they interpret particular events. Some people will favourably react to a private company providing a service, others to a state-owned company or agency – even if they are offering roughly the same services. Religious beliefs may affect people's opinion about a restaurant (not eating pork or beef; being vegetarian, etc.) so that they might not make a dispassionate judgement about the competence of the chef. A subsidiary of a large organisation may be regarded with scorn by its fellow subsidiaries. People in big companies tend to look down on those in their small suppliers. All such influences mean that what look like facts to one person may not look like the same facts to others.

Or consider someone's reaction to an airline. If a past experience includes being exceptionally well treated, they are likely to think more favourably about that airline in comparison to someone else who was perhaps refused boarding by the same company for being late. They may carry these feelings for years.

All these factors add up to a set of assumptions that each of us carry with us, influencing every waking moment in ways we usually don't think about. If we make assumptions without considering them we are likely to come to some very wrong conclusions.

Use the trials to uncover assumptions as well as testing theories

It's impossible to improve without changing.
Anon

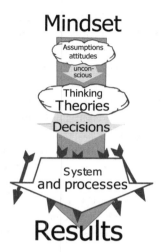

We all have prior experiences, culture and assumptions that we don't even think about, as well – perhaps – as more obvious ones which we do acknowledge. They influence our judgement and decisions. It's part of your job as a leader of change to use the evidence that arises in the planning and execution of the trial to enable people, including perhaps yourself, to reconsider how their assumptions affect their interpretation of theories of cause and effect.

When someone asserts that something is common sense, that's the time to be on the alert. Whose assumptions are in play, whose values, experience, skills make it common sense? In the 1990s it was widely thought to be common sense that profitable high-street computer retailing was impossible – until Apple started to open their stores and demonstrated otherwise.

Let's take the goal of being 'on target with minimum variation' as an example. We find it is a powerful aid in thinking about the ambition for a process, and in monitoring everyday progress. However, when first proposed to an audience brought up on achieving traditional 'OK/Not OK' targets it can generate a lot of resistance and scepticism. People have probably become accustomed to cutting costs and tolerating or ignoring complaints, and never considered it worthwhile to pay attention to variation in performance if it is within the specification. It may need repeated exploration to appreciate the theories behind the value of looking at all process variation, but at least these theories can be defined. But people are probably not even aware of the assumptions behind the mindset of judging only pass and fail criteria at work. It's just how it's always been, even though they almost certainly don't behave like that at home. Both might seem like common sense in their separate worlds, and rationalising them can be surprisingly difficult.

Considering all of these socio-emotional and political factors you might well agree with many of our clients who guess that aspects in the bottom part of the hamburger model might amount to ninety per cent of the reasons for failure in projects. Whatever the numbers in any particular case, it is certainly everyone's experience that an apparently well-planned project, using tools and techniques proven over many decades, can still founder on hard-to-define interpersonal issues or organisational politics.

The only way to make progress, though, is to actually get on and 'do' something different, following PDSA of course, and then find out about the effect. Thinking and talking do indeed have limits.

Plan the trials with the whole hamburger model in mind
For all that it may be impossible to exactly define what went wrong in the socio-emotional aspects of past projects, there are a number of ways you can increase the chance of success for future work.

Make sure this first trial relates to an immediate, relevant problem
As we suggested in Chapter 2, select a problem that looks as though it can be resolved without having to stray from your department too much, ideally something that can be changed within days and where a month or so will provide several cycles of operation. In this way everyone can see multiple data points, although five or six sometimes have to suffice to start with. Bigger issues need to wait until you have had some practice, have built credibility and understand the barriers as a result of actual work, not just planning or discussion.

Clear your lines with stakeholders
Determine with your team who they consider to be the most important customers, suppliers, allies, opponents. Agree on how to approach them to explain what you intend to do and why, and to ask for support if needed. Not

all will respond positively – such is the nature of scepticism or even cynicism – but in our experience it's better to make the attempt than to ignore them.

Explain that you would like to invite them to some of the meetings as the trials progress. At this stage you probably don't know when that will be, but it's great for both the team and visitors if stakeholders participate in discussions about options, or appreciate success and learning.

Select the right team for the trials and think about facilitation

Depending upon the issue, you need a mix of people who know the real work, have technical knowledge, and who represent the customers and suppliers. At least some of them need to be volunteers, optimistic and with a good sense of humour (GSOH), as it says on the dating adverts. If your organisation has a change-agent resource you have no doubt met some of them already, and will know whether you want to use them. Your team meetings will need facilitation, so ideally the change agents should be good at that. Make sure they don't see themselves primarily as technical experts who know best – a sure way to irritate their colleagues and clients. The politics of the project (the bottom part of the hamburger) need facilitation; the details of the methods and technologies in the top part should be chosen after due consideration, not predetermined.

Ensure the meeting processes are exemplary

Clarify at the first meeting what good facilitation actually is, even if some people have been exposed to it.

A good facilitator should:

- Be neutral and objective.
- Encourage everyone to participate.
- Provide feedback on the team's effectiveness.
- Challenge the team to deal with uncomfortable issues.
- Provide guidance without directing.
- Keep the team on track without controlling, including starting and finishing on time (though that may need authority too).
- Help the team work together to achieve their objectives.
- Encourage the development of team ground rules and appropriately use these to help the team move forward.
- Assist in reaching consensus without directing.
- Listen.

However, don't forget that this is your initiative. The facilitator is there to help you lead your team to achieve the objectives. On occasion you will need to be assertive and perhaps directive, so when you think this is necessary discuss with the facilitator offline how to approach it. Although you would like the facilitator to be energetic, don't let them take over.

The first meeting

The team probably won't be all the same people you worked with, as described in the last chapter, so this first meeting is another chance to make a first impression.

It sets the scene for the whole trial. This team is going to be interacting a lot, on the task itself as well as in the meeting room or over conference calls. Hence you need to take them through the approach you intend that they should use, one based upon the Three-Question Model.

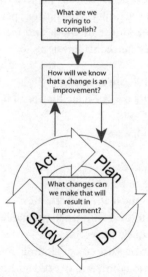

You should use the meeting disciplines as at the earlier meeting explained in Chapter 2, but adapted as you learn more about how they are received, and no doubt to in response to suggestions from the team members. This should then become the required style for meetings, whether you are present or not.

Use appropriate decision-making styles

Different circumstances require different approaches to making decisions. In a fire the fire marshal must direct people, regardless of rank or position, to behave in a particular way and do so urgently. Or there may be policy circumstances, such as employment issues, where you will have to insist on compliance with a particular approach.

In the improvement and change field it is rare for important decisions to be obvious. You may need to select from one of several options that look possible to some of the team but not to others. A quick decision probably means that dissenting views were not heard or that inconvenient data were brushed over. In this pilot study, and even more so during implementations into everyday operations, you need everyone involved to be supporting the direction taken, even if they have some reservations. Half-hearted support or toleration will not give you the best chance of success.

Getting everyone's support, even if some do have reservations, is building consensus and is likely to become increasingly important as complexity mounts. To reach a consensus that really is a consensus takes time. People need to feel that they have enough information, and that their voices were heard during the discussion process. This may need more time away from the meeting to allow for more data to be gathered, or simply to come to terms with adopting a different course to the one they initially favoured. Allowing this time may not be easy. However, as consensus decision making has a bit of a bad name with some people, with its connotations of endless discussions and fudge, it is well worth being prepared to take the time and to be methodical with decision-making processes.

Many of the tools of quality improvement build consensus when used properly, in an open collaborative manner. Here are a few examples:

- Jointly drawing up flowcharts shows how things are, or how people want them to be.
- Displaying honest data in run charts and talking through it openly enables people to feel involved, and feel that they understand what the issues are.
- Taking the next step of using control chart limits, which define the difference between noise and signals in the variation, is priceless in understanding whether a change in operation has resulted in a real change in output.

- Generating ideas on sticky notes by writing silently is a very powerful way of soliciting views that people may not be prepared to say aloud.

Taking the time to get everyone on the same page can seem wasted to those who live and breathe the issue being dealt with. You will need to ask for patience and show it yourself, which is likely to be tough on occasion. Our experience is that time taken at this stage will be rewarded with less time being wasted later on because someone felt left out or overridden. No one can measure the loss of emotional commitment that results from gloomy sessions over drinks, but good consensus decision making reduces it.

Leading the activities for the trial(s)

> Before you base a law on a case, test it two or three times and see whether the tests produce the same effects … this experiment should be made many times so that no accident may occur to hinder or falsify the proof…
> **Leonardo da Vinci, 1452–1519**

Leonardo and generations of other thinkers, academics and philosophers have had an easier job in many ways than yours. They could do their experiments away from the real world and with few consequences except frustration if things went wrong. The trials you undertake will almost certainly have to take place in the workplace, possibly with real products or services for real users or customers. It's often not possible to create a laboratory offline. This means that you should ensure the trials are set up carefully and that provision is made to avoid passing on failures to the customer. Thus you should initially run only one trial at a time, and pay it close attention. Once you have developed a culture of safety in the operation of trials, you can become more ambitious in both numbers and scope – but you will never regret starting at a scale that you can witness.

After planning the tests, making sure that theories and predictions have been made explicit, the following are some approaches and tools that increase the chance of success:

- Use meeting management disciplines, as explained earlier.
- Agree a team frequency, make it public and stick to it. This will determine the rhythm of the work and hence the overall pace. Having to get something done by the next meeting is a powerful motivator. Make sure the same people attend, seeking the support of your boss to clear time for people from other departments if necessary. (See below for an example of contingency planning.)
- Continually check and increase everyone's readiness to change by sharing your diagnosis about the unacceptability of the current situation, the attraction and benefits of the ambition, and giving your active support in the risky change activities. Nearly all are risky at first, one of many reasons why you should have only one or two small projects at his stage. Be aware also that your initial diagnosis may not be right, and be prepared not to be defensive if that's the case. Some recent data has shown that medical 'clinicians who were "completely certain" of their diagnosis ante mortem were shown to be wrong 40% of the time' when tested by post mortem examinations.[2] In problem solving and improvement we should all be aware of the need to propose theories and then to accept that the evidence should be the deciding factor on whether the theory is useful, not the strength of the argument presented or the seniority of the person advocating them.
- Take care to keep records from the start on the existing state of the process. These can range from data or written or recorded comments to videos, photographs, documents, etc. You will be amazed at how quickly you and everyone else forgets just how bad it was, and it undervalues achievements if you don't capture the starting point.
- Develop a project flowchart for the trial, and a Gantt chart to summarise the timing. These are powerful tools and if you have not already had some training, get some organised for yourself and others.
- Develop flowcharts and other graphic representations of the processes and put them on display, use them as the basis for discussion at the workplace.
- Discover measures that show what's going on in the process, as it runs. Make sure these measure variation if at all possible, not

---

2   From *Thinking Fast and Slow* by Daniel Kahneman, p263, Penguin Books 2011

just pass or fail (OK / Not OK) data. They need to correlate with important results, so that when they indicate that the process is stable you can be confident that the results will be as expected.

- Collect the data that arises during the trials as it really seems to be. This may be difficult if there has been a culture of targets, budgets and forecasts, possibly with bonuses or appraisals riding on the numbers. If this is the culture there may have been pressure to try to make the data fit the target, and this may have become the default, particularly if it is never talked about or investigated. Many of our clients find that their data are not robust when they start to analyse it for learning and improvement. We have seen measurement variation that turns out to be more than the basic process variation. Some records have an optimistic bias, some pessimistic; some biases will vary from shift to shift and so on. Particularly in call centre environments, data that are entered during the call may be so hard to get that the operator simply fills in a plausible number or reason. The distant analyst at their laptop comes to some conclusions regardless of the validity of the data and everyone is happy… So you need to be aware that a significant shift in attitude to collecting data is likely to be needed for the trials, and this can become quite politicised.

- Plot the data on run charts, and if the expertise is present, on control charts[3] that show how much variation is happening, and how to reliably distinguish signals from noise.

- Inspect all the output necessary so as to protect the customer from surprises.

- Aim to get the process predictable as the first step. Most processes that have not recently been worked on will be affected by multiple factors that make them unpredictable. Eliminating these causes of unpredictability one by one should take priority. Once the process has some predictability you have a better basis for making changes to improve it, and no doubt will be impatient to start doing so.

- Until a process is predictable no one can really know if a change is improvement; a better result may be down to luck. Just getting it stable is usually well worth doing on its own at first.

---

3 A control chart or process behaviour chart represents the natural variation of the process by dotted lines that help determine whether a change should be considered a surprise (an assignable cause) or not. You should ensure you get practical training to be able to understand and use control charts.

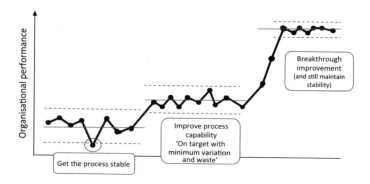

- Are there some immediate improvements to get on with? As mentioned before, these may be obvious things like broken equipment, multiple signoffs and safety compliance. Make a list of all of them, then prioritise by seriousness, urgency, cost and so on, and get on with it. You may also find it worth instigating some organising activities in the workplace, and there are various 'Lean' tools to help with this. However, you need to recognise that people generally don't make things disorganised on purpose; there's more to it than that. It's relatively easy to have a spring clean, but if the leadership doesn't understand how to maintain it things will slowly revert to the old ways. Ideally you will introduce structured workplace management as part of the changes that improve how the work works, and ensure that daily supervision knows how to keep things up to the new standard. See Chapter 5 for more on implementation.
- Try one change to a process at a time, until you can see the effect.

> The shortest way to do many things is to do only one thing at once.
> **Samuel Smiles, writer, 1812–1904**

Multiple changes reduce the validity of the conclusions you make. This policy may feel like it is slowing things down, but it is much more robust.
- Since there are likely to be several occasions when things can go wrong, you should develop the habit of actively planning for it. This contingency analysis table can be developed in a few minutes, and can save a lot of doubt later:

What could go wrong?	What can we do to prevent it?	How do we know if the preventative step is in place?	What shall we do if it goes wrong anyway?
Key person is off at the time of a trial	Check calendar for holidays, training, etc.	Confirm with individuals	Identify a stand-in, ensure they are prepared
	Agree with their boss that they are not to be called away	Note received from boss acknowledging the arrangement	

- Be prepared for surprises to emerge. Building on the metaphor we explored earlier in Chapter 1, in the forest of your department, where trees were falling but no one heard them, during this trial period there will be a lot more people listening! You should be ready for new knowledge to emerge, and this will set a pattern for all your improvement work. The more you learn the more you will discover about aspects of the work that never occurred to you to even consider. Make notes; add such insight to your general diagnosis. In our experience you should be prepared for surprises for up to a year after taking on a new role; many stresses emerge at different points of the natural or business calendar. Friendly old hands can help you to avoid the obvious ones, but you will have to ask.

- Remember also that the trial is an artificial situation. People behave differently when they have been paid attention to and are aware they are being watched. No chance of a tree falling without being heard in a trial, so to that degree it's a bit special.

- As the trials progress, arrange for your boss to attend some meetings in order to hear summaries and understand progress, barriers and prospects. Take the opportunity to be as clear as possible about costs and use these occasions to gain support for ongoing commitments.

- One trial is not likely to be enough, as Leonardo observed centuries ago. Make sure you do several, considering the time and resources available; there should be enough to cover a representative cross-section of the variety that the process experiences.

Ann's reflections

The trial was done. Ann shuffled the papers, flipcharts and pictures, looked again at the data, bringing it all together for the review meeting. She was bringing this team together for probably the last time, there would need to be some changes as they moved into implementation after the review.

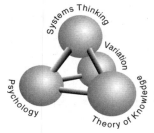

She was doing her best to capture the learning – there had been some useful lessons so that future trials would be better – but she was also thinking through the situation in terms of the System of Profound Knowledge again.

Systems thinking:

- There had been a shift in thinking about the purpose of the work, moving it more towards customer factors.
- They still hadn't got to the bottom of the flows through the processes; some incidents were so rare that they hadn't happened since they started the project.
- The changes she was planning were still just patches, really; there would need to be more work to get the variation out altogether.
- Her colleagues had been impressed with the efforts and were glad to see the issues being taken seriously.

Variation:

There was still going to be more variation and no one knew how much, so all they were really doing was planning to mitigate it.

They were getting better at identifying useful measures, thanks to spending more time observing what was going on. Ann could see how this would continue provided she kept up the interest, but she had to guard against everything being buried in spreadsheets; she wanted the data visible.

Theory of knowledge:
- There had been a few 'ah-ha' moments, not least that they could actually make a prediction of the effects of language confusion and thus begin to justify some investment in translating instructions. No one had really taken this seriously before, and minority communities seemed to be less satisfied than others.
- Some of the team had been suitably sobered when they visited a site that had developed display boards in the office, and realised that they didn't know about it. This could encourage more sharing of learning in future, but it wouldn't happen without her attention, she was sure.
- Theories are being discussed, which was progress, but many managers still seemed to want to rush into action on the basis of just one result – and that needed watching out for.

Psychology:
- There had been a welcome for the trouble taken to communicate but scepticism that it would be kept up.
- She guessed it was too early to hope for a pull for more change, but she was still a bit disappointed that some supervisors seemed to think that this one project would be enough.
- Her own colleagues had mixed reactions; for every enthusiast there seemed to be another sceptic, and one or two were just uncooperative.

She turned to her ideas about the preparation and structure of the review workshop.

4 Making sense of the results

Study the past if you would divine the future.
Confucius, 6th century BCE

Ann's story

Four weeks later, and the world already seemed a very different place. Ann could see that before the problem-solving activities started she had been preoccupied with rather superficial issues: how to create the right impression, the sort of impact she was making. Incidents, ranging from the sweepstake in the drawer to her irritation on the mechanics of the meeting room, had unsettled her although she had not wanted to admit it. But now, with a month of data from operations she had to some extent witnessed, and the discussions and activities of the work, she was getting a better sense of proportion.

People had liked her approach of drawing out their part of the organisation as a system, and clarifying its purpose. She had several comments such as 'now I see where we fit in' and 'I never realised our priorities should be aimed at doing the right things for the customers'. The team had come up with some good ideas for intercepting the mail to ensure that letters made sense. There were a lot to sift through, and this would not be the long-term solution, but they felt like steps in the right direction.

There had been some resistance, though. A couple of her offices had become part of the organisation only recently as a result of a takeover, and felt let down by a previous change initiative. They seemed to feel that their views had been ignored then, and weren't ready to open up about their problems. Her boss, too, was not being easy. He said the right things about supporting her attempts to be methodical, testing theories and having enough evidence, but seemed to be intimidated by the financial director. When new forecasts had been required for a revised budget she felt he had taken the easy route, agreeing economies without having any idea how they would be reached. She felt she might be exposed as being a bit too different if she could not create improvements quickly, and that any extra money agreed now might be withdrawn when the next budget was being squeezed.

> But the ideas for identifying the compensation letters were good and she was impressed. Now she needed to get them turned into routine processes, even if just for a few months until bigger changes could be developed and the fixes would no longer be necessary.

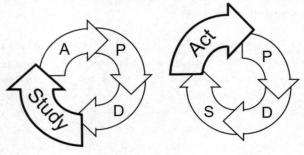

How did the theories stand up to the test?

By this stage, from looking around your work to the carrying out of experiments, you have completed one revolution of the PDSA Cycle. You can see why, in spite of the sequence of its initials, the Cycle should start with Study. The first Study was followed by Act: decisions about where to put the first improvement efforts. Plan surfaced theories of cause and effect, with predictions of what was hoped for from the trials in terms of process and results data. Without these predictions there would have been nothing to compare with. Do was the trials to see how the theories work out in practice.

So we come to the second Study. This is a crunch point in generating learning that can be applied to the benefit of the organisation, both in terms of improving how the work will work, and in how the trials were conducted. A review meeting is needed to confirm the changes that need to be made.

You will need to take care that this review does not get infected with what is probably the default way of reviewing departmental or project activities and data. In the vast majority of performance reviews there is a drive to satisfy some external agency, such as the boss, the parent company or perhaps a regulator. There is probably some target that needs to be hit. In subsequent ongoing work, numbers that come out just the good side of the target are received with relief; the report can be completed and the meeting closed without too much discussion. Numbers that cannot be massaged to be on the good side will probably lead to recriminations. Much time may be spent adjusting the figures to give the impression of a favourable outcome, or in producing plausible explanations to shift the blame if that's not possible. In either case a depressingly small amount of time is spent on learning about the process or project with a view to improving it.

You might need to make this review explicitly different. It must not be seen as a judgement meeting, an equivalent of a legal trial with everyone ready to defend their role or pass the blame to others. It is part of a continual learning process, a second Study, to help you and the participants make decisions for improvement. You will find that data that surprised the team is much more useful than numbers which might have come out exactly as predicted. Surprises give the possibility of new knowledge, whereas a trial that ran as predicted means that someone already knew the answer. Or that the data are not so clean after all.

As the trial progresses, and coming up to this decision-making review meeting, it may be hard to prevent outsiders from taking advantage of the growing knowledge, perhaps in pressing for immediate implementation on a broad scale. This is why the preparation described at the start of the project is important, getting stakeholders such as the boss and the customers to agree to help. At this stage you may need to appeal to them to give you some space and time.

The review meeting

We have suggested that this should be structured separately from the project team meetings. It has a different purpose, which is to come to conclusions and propose or authorise changes in the ongoing work. This may require other participants as well as the problem-solving team.

Here are some important factors in conducting a successful review meeting:

- Be explicit about its two purposes:
  - To study the outcomes of the trial, so see how the changes should be taken further.
  - To study the process of the problem-solving work to see what worked well, what didn't, and what is needed for the future.

● Be exemplary in the meeting management process. You have been using it several times, and it will be familiar to the regular team members. If there are new attendees they need to be taken through the rationale at the start, and to commit to supporting it.

● Get the team to prepare summaries on displays that can be put on the wall, in big writing that can be read from a couple of metres away. You want attendees to stand around them and discuss, not just listen to presentations. Make sure the story is coherent through the displays, so that non participants can make sense of what was done.

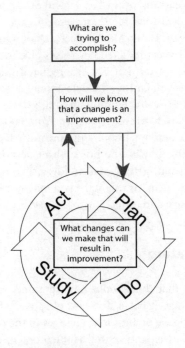

● Use the Three-Question Model and perhaps make a presentation to explain it at the opening part of the meeting:
  ◆ What you set out to accomplish.
  ◆ How you decided you would judge whether the changes were actually improvements.
  ◆ What the team intended to do, and what it actually did.

● Display the data in graphic form, using control charts if you can, so that attendees can see how the variation has changed. If it has not changed it should still be shown, and will influence the decisions you are to make.

- Ask the visitors to respond to the displays by:
  - ◆ Appreciating the work done, and the ideas.
  - ◆ Offering comments on the conclusions.
  - ◆ Offering their support in making things happen or asking how they can help.
- There are three categories of decision (Acts) that can emerge from the meeting:
  - ◆ **Adopt.** The results showed an improvement and the methods of working look practical. Adopt the changes and implement in everyday operations. This requires an implementation plan, as discussed in Chapter 5. If this is the case and there is any doubt about your confidence, consider looking for further validation, by re-running the test with the changes taken away again. If they were useful changes the problem should reappear; if it does not, the initial tests were maybe just lucky and you still haven't found the cause. If you are a supplier to some automotive manufacturers you may be required to show you have done this validation. As shown by Leonardo's quote in Chapter 3, this is not a new idea, but it is still rare.
  - ◆ **Adapt.** The results were unclear; maybe the changes need to involve other parts of the organisation. Adapt the trials and retest with changes.
  - ◆ **Abandon.** The trials indicate that the proposed new approach does not help at all, or perhaps the improvement is too small to justify the effort in changing. This may call for the team to be wound up, and starting all over again. Such a decision is of course tough for the leaders, but it's much better to come clean about it and not to carry on meeting and working without any real prospect of improvement. You and the team members will have learned from the work, and this learning is best applied to the next problem on the list. Getting a positive result will be more likely as a consequence.
- After the decisions about the project and next steps have been agreed, conduct a proper review of the problem-solving activities, both in the events in the workplace as the trial progressed, and in the planning and meeting processes. The Four-Student Model outlined

in Chapter 1 is the basis for this. Everyone should be interested in finding out if the problem solving works well when you do it properly, as opposed to not working if you are disorganised. Or, possibly, if you did it properly but it didn't work well, or if it worked despite you being disorganised. The only secure route for the future is to find an approach that does a good job for you when you use it properly, and then use it.

A simple series of questions on each aspect will generate a lot of useful information:

◆ How did what you actually do differ from what you planned?
◆ What went well?
◆ What didn't go so well?
◆ What training needs have been identified?
◆ What would be done differently next time?

Most of these questions relate of course to socio-emotional factors – the bottom part of the hamburger model.

● Generate the responses, ideally by each attendee writing separately in silence on sticky notes. Then collect the notes and arrange a separate meeting to digest them and agree actions.[4]

● At the close of the meeting carry out a careful action listing which should include a communication plan:

◆ What are you going to say to and ask of your people?
◆ What are you going to say to and ask of your boss and stakeholders?
◆ What are you going to say to and ask of your colleagues?

● When considering who should be involved with making presentations outside the meeting, think about asking a sceptic rather than a known enthusiast. If they agree it may make them think and help their own approach. But don't choose a cynic – that would probably be too high a risk!

● And it should go without saying that the meeting should conclude with a meeting review.

You need to consider what to do with the team, and the hopes and expectations of the individuals. Those who have contributed well are candidates for future projects, and for training in the methods and tools. A

---

4 This is a variety of the affinity diagram technique.

comment should go onto their personnel records. Look for opportunities for them to present to conferences, either within the company or to trade or management associations. Such recognition will be remembered for a long time, and will bolster you own credibility too.

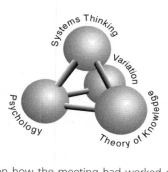

Ann pondered on how the meeting had worked once more. She was ready to run PDSA once again to progressively implement the changes, and learn more about how the people in the organisation respond to change in general – but before that came the lessons.

Systems thinking:

- There had been quite a buzz across all the attendees as they enjoyed using the same language and realised they could help each other.
- They could see that there would also be implications for others who were not there, and were slightly nervous about getting them onside because they hadn't shared the experience.
- She felt there must be many quite similar processes elsewhere in the company that could take advantage of their learning, but the existing culture didn't really encourage that. In fact, there was a bit of history of resentment towards anyone who thought they could apply their lessons to someone else, so she would have to tread carefully.
- She was satisfied that they had worked up a good plan in the form of a flowchart with dates and reporting times.

Variation:
- She noted she needed to remember that this plan was just about mitigation, and that she would need to escalate to get the resources to make fundamental changes. This was becoming a preoccupation.
- The measures looked useful, and given the high-profile consequences of errors getting through to the press office if they were not, she hoped they were right. Time would tell.
- They still hadn't got to the bottom of getting results recorded without bias.

Theory of knowledge:
- The whole process of sharing theories about what was going on and what they were going to attempt in future had gone down well. People were increasingly talking about theories; now she had to make sure it didn't stop there. It had to become practice that worked.
- She was satisfied she had checked with all the key stakeholders to try and make sure they understood the goals and the intentions – operational definitions were also becoming a common reference point.

Psychology:
- They had held a thank-you party, and her boss had turned up; when she next went to Mumbai she would need to repeat it. Also, several supervisors had volunteered for out of hours meetings without expecting overtime.
- She had a good feeling about a couple of the supervisors who had worked on the trial and who would be closely involved going forward. There could be opportunities to widen their roles in a few months.

5 Implementing Improvements

A leaf that is destined to grow large has grooves and wrinkles
in it at the start. Now if one has no patience and wants it
smooth like a willow leaf, there is trouble ahead.
Goethe, German writer, 1749–1832

Ann's story

The review meeting had gone well, better than Ann had hoped. The
recommendations were in themselves not complicated, consisting of an
extra step of inspection before letters were posted. If a payment was being
made without an explanation, then the clerk would refer back to the case file
and create a manual letter. It appeared that the reason for the earlier problems
was that the great majority of payments were being sent with covering letters,
and managers did not take seriously the few reports of failures. However, no
one seemed to know why a few had been slipping through, or exactly how
many were doing so. This would take more investigation.

Meanwhile there was the task of making the changes in two big locations
and several smaller ones, with implications for staff rotas and training. Her
boss had accepted the need or the changes, and the group press officer
was relieved that there might be an end in sight to referrals from the media.
As far as he was concerned it did not matter if most of the payments were
correct; the small number that reached him caused a disproportionate
amount of trouble. And Ann had still not been able to find out why some
of the subsequent complaints about the lack of a letter had not been dealt
with properly in her department. It looked as if some managers were not
prepared to admit their function's role in these failures.

So she was looking forward to the implementation planning meeting
at last, and to seeing the numbers improve. Next week she was to have a
meeting with Group IT to see what their attitude would be to the changes,
and to the longer-term needs. Getting to the bottom of the variation
between sites and categories of complaints would have to come later, after
the customers had been protected in the short term, but she wanted to see
what the scale would likely be.

Implement improvements and stabilise (PDSA)

At this stage the full significance of multiple rapid cycles of PDSA will become increasingly evident, as learning accumulates and mistakes are caught before they become too serious. However the contrast with traditional methods may cause discomfort and resistance. Participants and stakeholders are often used to impressive schedules for rolling out changes and don't recognise the damage this apparent predictability causes. However controlled we would like the implementation to be, natural variation across a human system means it will have to be adapted to some hard-to-predict extent. We have talked at length about PDSA in exploration and testing; now it shows its strengths for implementation projects.

Implementing change is uncertain

> In planning for battle I have always found that plans are
> useless, but planning is indispensible.
> **Dwight D Eisenhower, 1890–1969**

Successful military leaders have learned that they need to understand what the goals have to be, to prepare resources and a series of steps to get there, and to allow for contingencies when things go wrong. But they also know they must expect to be surprised because they can't be sure what will go wrong, and to be ready to learn from the experiences, adjusting tomorrow's activities as needed. Managers of organisational change should follow this example, and be wary of simple formulae. Predicting the future is always an approximate skill. The best way to deal with surprises is to expect some and have agreed ways to acknowledge them and respond – not to proceed in the blind hope that it will all be OK.

You will almost certainly have come across projects or programmes that talk of 'roadmaps', 'cascades', or 'rollouts'. The Six Sigma model (discussed in Chapter 8) has two stages, 'Improve' followed by 'Control'. Such language makes implementation seem rather simple, as if hard work or top management pressure alone will make things happen faster. Much project management thinking seems dominated by research and planning of the project, in particular about 'critical paths' and 'work packages'. It tends to be light on learning during the project. Why shouldn't your implementation be similarly straightforward?

The answer lies in the nature of change leadership in comparison with management of tangible, physical projects. A civil engineering project, for instance, is rightly dominated by the imperatives of achieving the target on time, on cost, and with many other defined requirements, such as safety and environmental issues. If you read about a major civil engineering project you will be able to find predictions for when, say, a machine will complete its tunnelling work, years in advance. There will of course be uncertainties on the way, but with a highly competent leadership team you can be pretty confident they will adjust to surprises and force the work on. They will have contingency funds to reallocate resources, and clarity of definition in the goal which means that everyone knows their role. In addition, the managers are specialists in planning and controlling resources to a timeline, so although they may meet new problems they have the benefit of experience in having overcome such barriers before.

Problem solving, process improvement and transformation work is different. It can never be about forcing change. It's primarily about helping people to be ready to change how they behave. Anyone can be instructed, but no one has to follow unless they want to. You and your colleagues have to find out what is the best way to increase this readiness to change in every circumstance you encounter. Your goals are probably less tangible than a construction project and their achievement is unlikely to be made more likely by more pressure – indeed, pressure can be counterproductive. This is not to say that a sense of urgency is not important; it's to assert that you are responsible for leading, not just managing, the change, being ahead of the pack, experiencing the barriers and discovering how to get them lifted. Then you can hope that people will follow your example.

Having a good plan is just the start
Acceptance of a degree of uncertainty is therefore critical to the success of this and every other change that you lead. Nobody has done previously the task you are about to undertake. No one has been exactly where you

are; nobody has ever been trying to get exactly to the goals you have agreed. There is no plan that you can copy and paste.

In planning your implementation you can and should do a thorough preparation job, clarifying goals, estimating timings, resource needs, training and so on. You should ask others about their experiences, discuss possible problems and develop contingency plans to deal with them. But you should always expect the unexpected, seek to detect it as soon as possible, make it visible, and rotate the PDSA cycle again and again as the discipline for learning on the way.

The process of implementing changes

Meetings are always about increasing readiness to change

The implementation team must contain the line managers and supervisors of the area affected by the changes. This should not be fudged, no matter how much they may claim they haven't got time for meetings. At this stage, with the project in your own department, you can insist on this. Anyone who suggests that they send a deputy for a meeting for planning changes in their function is indicating that they don't think it's important. Their staff will take the lead from their boss, and will quickly interpret any tendency to downplay any priorities.

Meeting management processes should be exemplary (again, are you surprised?). As with the exploration, problem solving and review stages, the meetings are the one component that you can definitively lead and ensure they are conducted as you wish. All of the guidelines outlined in Chapter 2 remain valid, with a particular emphasis on time management as many of the delegates will necessarily be called off their regular jobs and will not appreciate being delayed. You are likely to find this meeting discipline tested; some line managers have so far been able to observe your investigation and planning work from a distance, and may hope that if they keep their head down it will all go away. As they find themselves pinned down, asked for commitments or even asked to behave differently, there will be many ways they might prevaricate. Hopefully your problem-solving team contained attendees from the areas being affected by the changes and they will be ambassadors for the solutions, but that cannot always be the case.

Each meeting will therefore need to contain elements of increasing readiness to change. The emphasis will depend upon attendees' previous exposure. In the first place you must build their awareness of the degree of dissatisfaction about the current situation; you cannot assume they have accepted or even heard of the previous work you have done.

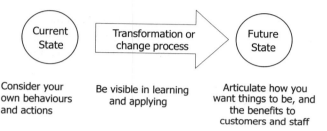

Consider your own behaviours and actions

Be visible in learning and applying

Articulate how you want things to be, and the benefits to customers and staff

Next, clarify with them the goals that were developed in the review stage of the problem-solving work, and refine them with this audience – the people who are closest to the routine work ahead.

The third component is to build the change process with them, the precise steps that are intended to ensure that the new ways of working have the best possible chance of being reliably and quickly adopted.

> He that will not apply new remedies must expect new evils, for time is a great innovator.
> **Francis Bacon, philosopher, 1561–1626**

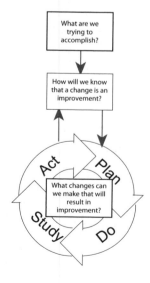

You will find that the Three-Question Model is once again a very useful basis for planning the introduction of the changes into everyday operations, as shown in this rather basic illustration.

1. To reduce the chance of errors arising from customer queries, and to deal more effectively with any that are not properly resolved.
2. Counting the numbers of errors or complaints. Keeping track of the costs of the change.
3. Change the work instructions, train the operators, inform others affected, collect data.

Test theories of implementation

You should test the implementation using PDSA, just as you tested options for addressing the problem in chapter 3. The value of tests of implementations lies in their exposure of deeper and deeper issues each time they are run. If you have many people involved in the work – perhaps on shifts, in different locations, perhaps employed by third parties – or there are different service or product groups, then there will need to be adjustments to some extent. Only by using PDSA will these variations be regarded as planned learning rather than surfacing at some stage as apparent failures.

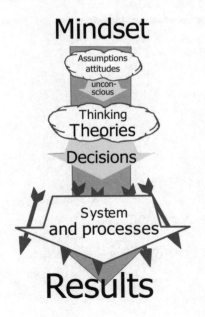

As this diagram shows, behind the work processes operating every day lie decisions taken months or years ago. If they were taken by people who are no longer with the organisation there may be little resistance to doing things differently, but if some of today's managers were part of the original decisions they may still feel committed to how things should be done. The resulting opposition may not emerge visibly; it may need to be teased out and people's feelings recognised and responded to.

Multiple PDSAs, conducted rapidly, will flush out both positive and negative feedback each time, until eventually you can hope to surface why things are as they are. There are similarities with your own fitness or diet regime, the roots of which probably lie many years back and can take a lot of work to dig out and discard.

Planning for everyday standard operations

These suggestions are made to help you avoid the trap of making valid changes that fail to become part of everyday work, everywhere.

Involve process owners

In your earlier investigations you will have found out whether the processes being dealt with have process owners. If there are such people you will hopefully already have been collaborating with them, and they will be members of the stakeholder group. If you have only just found out that they exist, now is certainly the time to consult. This uncertainty is a consequence of the extremely wide variety of interpretation of the role of the process owner, and of their profile.

Work with the Process Management Cycle

The Process Management Cycle provides a structure that starts with the design and implementation of standard ways of working, but incorporates continual monitoring and change so the operation does not fossilise.

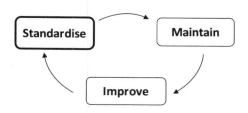

It could be assumed to be common sense that one should discover the best way to do the work and then make that the standard, but it is not common at all. One reason is a healthy scepticism about bureaucracy.

> It is an inevitable defect that bureaucrats care more for routine than results.
> **Walter Bagehot, economist, 1826–77**

Most of us will have experience that seems to support this attitude. However, it does not have to be so. The ways of working must not become a meaningless drudge to be persisted with regardless of the circumstances. That way leads to boredom for the operators and decline in performance, for the circumstances of the daily operations do not stay the same forever. All kinds of small changes, from technology problems to customer attitudes, will accumulate to degrade performance until some kind of crisis finally breaks.

When talking with friends about this aspect of making the work work, their response is often that it only applies to large organisations. However, our experience is that the need for repeatability does not respect the size of your function. In small offices, practices can vary widely depending upon who picks up the phone, orders the stationery, responds to a problem. Confusion, disappointment and cost are the consequences in a local business, just as they are in a multinational.

Developing standard ways of doing the everyday work
We are trying to develop a self-organising system, as far as possible. Good standardisation is an agreed way to do the work, supported by documents that identify both the steps that must be followed precisely and the steps that allow flexibility. It should convey the purpose of the process, its key steps and the customer requirements to bring a customer focus to all work. It should also clarify restrictions and constraints, as well as roles and responsibilities. If it does all these things well, the operators will take to it and the need for on-the-job supervision is reduced – to everyone's benefit.

Any improvement activity that developed new or modified processes should have worked with operators to define Standard Operating Procedures (SOPs), associated training processes and job descriptions. In principle, the description of the method should be in the form of a flowchart.

Standardisation thus needs engagement. It must not be seen as a set of rules that result in punishment or reprimands if not followed. Documented procedures created by managers or engineers and imposed on the workforce will probably not work. Nor is a procedure manual gathering dust on the shelf good standardisation, and there is also no point going into details about things that do not affect the outcome.

Four rules for standardisation help create a positive atmosphere for its implementation:

1. Standardise only the important factors that impact the product or service.
2. Process operators should understand the 'why' of the standardisation and be able to influence the process.
3. Managers and technical experts should play a support role to the process operators involved in maintaining and developing the process.
4. Process reviews are for learning and improvement, not reprimand.

Local managers carry the prime responsibility for ensuring that standard operations are made real. One aspect of this is a routine culture of operating according to the standard, not accepting bad inputs, not doing 'bad' work and not passing on 'bad' outputs, however they are defined and whatever their apparent origins. This is likely to be a radical shift from historic patterns of 'it's good enough, just get on with it'.

An integral part of ensuring the success of standard operations is to ensure that people have the skills and knowledge to carry out the work.

The robustness of standard operations is tested at times of pressure. Questions in case of trouble need to be based on process, not personality. Any manager who urges extra effort in time of trouble is in effect demonstrating lack of belief in the robustness of their operations, and should not be surprised if previous attempts to maintain standard operations are thus undermined. The methods in the standard operations guide should be regarded as being capable of improvement, but only after a disciplined approach to doing so.

We cover the subject of maintaining process performance in Chapters 6 and 7, and making step changes to improve it in Chapter 8.

Display and discuss process performance

The implementation team should work with the process supervisors and operators to develop display boards at the workplace. These should feature the position of the process in the organisation as a system, and express clearly its purpose and contribution to optimising this system.

The customers, suppliers and support processes should be identified, and key measures displayed on run charts or, again and preferably, on control charts. Some measures will be those that enumerate the results of this part of the work (this process); others will be indications of performance within the process – analytic data. Ideally the analytic data will show *effectiveness* – how well the process is working in comparison to its design. If these data are as expected the process should be *efficient*, and this will be indicated by the results data. It is very hard to run a process for efficiency, i.e. low cost, if it is not effective. Other relevant information such as training matrices, holiday plans and so on may be added, although care needs to be taken not to overwhelm the space.

A visual display board must be live, used at least weekly if not daily. It should be the focal point of briefing meetings, and the start point for explaining the process to visitors. Thus it is probably best for it to be done by hand rather than as a computer display, although live information on a screen may be a useful addition.

Keep the IT people on board through the changes

You may not have any changes that affect the IT function, but the chances are that something will need to be different eventually. If you develop a consistent policy of integrating IT people in your process development work you will find that both sides understand each other a little better. Programmers and analysts are often frustrated that line staff and supervisors do not see their work in systems terms, of flow and decisions, and have to make assumptions or guesses as a consequence. The more you and your people understand how the IT people think about work, and vice versa, the better will be any future IT project.

Communicate, communicate (and two way, not just broadcast)

Be sure that you make others who interact with your function aware of what you are doing, not just by broadcasting, but also by dialogue, using language – operational definitions – that they understand. This should include any changes you need from them, benefits for them or the organisation as a whole, and any risks for them.

This communication will become more important as time goes by. You may be managing in a different way to the way they have previously experienced, or you may appear to be trying an approach which has some history but encountered problems. You need other people to be at least neutral, even if not enthusiastic, about how you are making the work work better, and this requires them to know about it.

Consider your future role as a manager and leader

When you are recruited as a department manager the emphasis is generally on making the everyday work work properly. As shown on this graphic, this 'manage processes' is one of three principal roles of managers, with methodologies for understanding and maintaining performance.

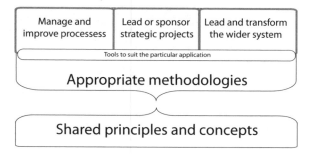

However, at the end of the problem-solving process described so far, you will have laid your personal foundations beyond maintenance, showing yourself capable of analysing and leading improvement as well as the routine. The principles and concepts we have been discussing are also applicable to improvement and strategic work, and the more you have become familiar with them at a rapid, local scale, the more confident you will feel when working across the system. There are different methodologies to be used as the issues change and escalate but many tools – such as flowcharting, data analysis or idea generation – are applicable in these differing circumstances.

We explore aspects of strategic change and organisational strategy in Chapters 8 and 9, but in the next chapter we look at the process management approach to maintaining the performance of your newly standardised work.

Ann stood up to close the implementation review meeting. In the beginning it hadn't been easy persuading all the supervisors that they would need to get everyone to take the extra inspection step. She wasn't really surprised as at first glance it would be extra work, and she had decided not to take up her boss's reluctant offer to fund some more people. The working group had only agreed after a lot of debate that the department might eventually have less reworking and fewer aggrieved calls from customers if they could avoid sending out unexplained payments, but that would not show immediately.

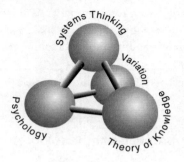

In addition, not everyone had felt that the effort in setting up workplace displays would be worthwhile. Ann suspected that some people were not carrying out regular briefings, and that others were nervous about doing it. It sounded as though communication training hadn't been very good, and the information provided from top management was intermittent. She had visited another local service centre as part of a regional business club, and they described a similar experience. Using this insight she had agreed that two out of the many work groups would act as pathfinders for the others. This should expose the underlying issues and be another demonstration of PDSA. She would need to go to Mumbai, where the outsourced management were lobbying to be paid more for their contribution. But this was not a bad thing; she wanted to visit them anyway, and she would also see the offices where they serviced other clients.

She moved the meeting to a close with the review once again: what had gone well, what concerns did people have?

Afterwards she stuck to her discipline of using the System of Profound Knowledge in considering the lessons from implementing. The picture was mixed; plenty to do differently next time.

Systems thinking:

- The Process Management Cycle had been well received as a sort of map for what would be coming later, when things settled down.
- They had managed the various work streams reasonably, and the previous care taken to inform the operational managers had been well worth the trouble. She paused with this one. Was it systems thinking or psychology, or a bit of both? No matter.

Variation:

- They had learned a lot about implementing in small as well as large locations, but there still seemed to be a lot of people who thought that standardisation should mean exactly the same everywhere. Another topic to revisit in future implementations.
- They had made a start in getting displays on the walls in a few offices, but who could know how much effort it would take to keep it up to date?

Theory of knowledge:

- Ann was somewhat depressed by people's ready use of clichés in the planning and review meetings. Talking of route maps and rollouts led people to think they just needed to put pressure on all the actions, and all would be well. Even 'deployment' and 'programme' seemed to lead to lots of time on the computers to map the supposed future, and nothing like enough flexibility when events didn't work out as forecast. Perhaps she should try 'campaign' in future. In spite of the military connotations, it did at least have aspects of uncertainty in it. The whole topic showed how the use of words could have consequences for behaviours.

Psychology:

- There had been, and probably still was, a clear difference in receptiveness to the new process in areas run by participants in the trial team, as opposed to those who had not been directly involved at that stage. They would need to pay more attention next time.

- The people in the areas implementing the change last had felt a little neglected, possibly taken for granted. That was another aspect to work more on next time – someone had to be last, but they should feel they got the same consideration as the early adopters.

6 Managing ongoing performance

The total disorder in the universe, as measured by the quantity that physicists call entropy, increases steadily over time.
Freeman Dyson, theoretical physicist, 1923 to date

Ann's story

Another month on, so much learning, and Ann wondered when surprises would stop jumping out at her. Someone had suggested that people doing her job didn't need to watch soap operas because real life was sometimes much odder than fiction. Last week she dealt with one of her managers in deep trouble: his bank was calling in the mortgage, apparently his wife had been spending the mortgage money on gambling, and he would have to resign. Both the HR manager and her boss had been out of contact and, since she had no one else to turn to, Ann had spoken to the bank and persuaded them to hold off long enough for the couple to work out some sort of plan. It had been a rewarding but exhausting afternoon. Nothing else got proper attention. But he was a good manager, and might well be an ally in future – or so she hoped.

Now she was on the plane back from Mumbai, itself an experience she would never forget. At home she felt she knew the rules of work, though frustrated by lack of energy and what looked like game playing in some of the supervision. In Mumbai there was energy everywhere and well-qualified staff, but also an almost irresistible force to change things every time some target or other seemed threatened. It didn't help that the people were employed by the outsourcing agency, and though they knew their stuff Ann had to go through the agency to influence the supervisors. Their senior managers had many clients to look after and Ann didn't feel that she mattered much. But there had been no doubt that taking the trouble to visit had made a big impression, and she loved the Indian welcome.

She was trying to work out how to come to terms with the need to better understand the whole situation – the relationships between home and overseas facilities and the customer needs. Even after several months she didn't feel close to grasping the various extremes of volume and urgency

> that came and went with the seasons. This learning was taking a lot of time. Somehow she needed to get more operations predictable, and keep them there, whilst uncovering the best candidates for major change.

Keeping the show on the road

Freeman Dyson's quote at the start of this chapter refers to entropy, a term not much heard in management circles but which goes on everywhere across the universe, for all time, whether we know about it or not. It is the tendency for the universe to become disordered. Mountains erode, complex life decomposes and stars explode. Or, to put another way, children's bedrooms become messy, gardens are overcome with weeds and cars break down. Or in yet another way, your work processes will become less suitable for the purpose than they used to be, maybe accumulating workarounds, or perhaps training doesn't keep up with recruitment. Entropy truly is everywhere.

Life is one of the ways nature creates order out of chaos, but only as long as life lasts. It requires energy, then it decays and it becomes disordered. We are all made of elements formed in stars, put together for the moment in a marvellous but temporary natural system.

Everyone knows this intuitively, of course: gardeners, parents, decorators and drivers. Just as soon as you have decorated the stairs and landing, the paintwork starts to lose its newness. Kids bang the wall, the vacuum cleaner chips the door, the dog leaves hair everywhere, the sun fades the carpet, someone spills coffee and dirt arrives on shoes. It takes an immense amount of effort to keep things as they were, as exemplified by the trouble taken in ancient palaces and galleries. Even with all this effort things slowly decay, and of course the wrong sort of restoration or preservation can actually make things worse.

Because we instinctively sense this deterioration most people tolerate it in their everyday life. We do our best to stave it off, but recognise that we have to keep a sense of proportion – well, hopefully we do! But our customers see no need to make any allowances. They deal with our organisation without any knowledge about whether it has been recently modernised and expect it to deliver regardless. If the system and processes are all new it should be relatively easy to make the work work effectively (well, hopefully, after any teething troubles, and if the processes were properly developed!). But the passage of time will inexorably lead to your processes becoming less effective unless energy is expended in restoring their original state. If energy hasn't been recently invested, it may be hard to live up to your customers' expectations, particularly if your competitors have been keeping up to date. You may have rework, workarounds, inspections and so on, all because the effort was not made to continually monitor and improve where it was seen to be needed. Entropy is winning.

Active process management is thus the approach we take to continually regenerate the organisation, preventing deterioration.

Pay end-to-end attention

By now you have explored most aspects of the process, learned how it works both day to day and under pressure, and picked up some tools that are useful in understanding and improving it. The graphic overleaf shows the flow of this understanding, and enables you to see what else to explore.

Use the Process Management Cycle to fight entropy

This section builds upon this overview and assumes that processes have been developed and standardised in accordance with the guidance in Chapter 5.

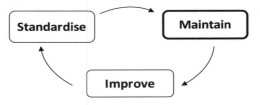

If you want to impress your customers with your products or services, you have to ensure that work is being done as intended and lead continual change as necessary to keep the output on target with minimum variation. Here are some key activities and processes that will help.

Use exemplary meeting management processes

This is clearly a repeating theme! But, as we said before, when you consider that it is at meetings that you have the most interaction with your own and other managers it is worth the effort to set the example. Every meeting is an opportunity to use PDSA to learn about how the work is working, and about how people are responding to your efforts.

Developing standard operations

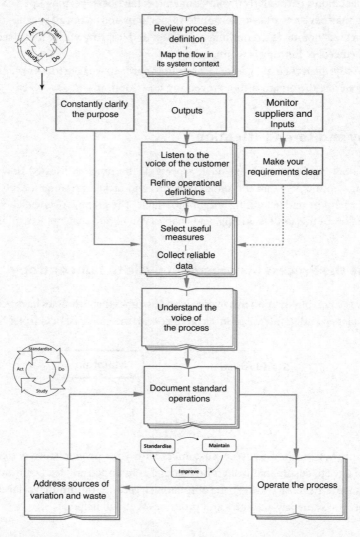

Even the shortest meeting should have an explicit purpose, a prepared agenda, use such appropriate tools as are known, be properly run, and have clear conclusions – which, in turn, should be reviewed at the start of the next one. Every meeting should briefly review the process of the meeting so that everyone sees the learning that emerges.

Carry out regular process reviews

If capable processes are operated according to standard operating procedures they should generate outputs that at least comply with customer needs. You therefore need to review the operations to see if standard procedures are being followed and if they are indeed producing the desired outputs. You should establish a review timetable and take advantage of the visual management systems to reassure yourself that all is as it should be. You should expect your managers to do the same.

Revisiting the metaphor of the forest and falling trees from Chapter 1, by doing these reviews you are increasing the chances that someone will be listening when a tree falls, and that learning can take place as a result.

The atmosphere of a process review needs to be one of learning and looking for evidence that, for instance, the process measures correlate to the results. It should be seen as continual Study, with the intention of identifying potential problems before they cause trouble. People should realise that their work is actually a continual series of experiments, with opportunities to learn from the assignable causes of variation as they are detected (see page 82).

A review needs to cover at least the following subjects, which you can use as a checklist to make sure you address each of them:

Topic	Comments
Are standard work instructions clear and being used?	
Is the workspace properly organised ('5S', see below)?	
Understand operational constraints on the work	
Look out for visual evidence of mistake-proofing precautions	
Is safety signage in place?	
Are health and safety requirements being observed?	

Other topics will no doubt emerge as you apply this list, and can be added.

How is variation being managed?

Given the generic aim of having the process 'on target with minimum variation', use any graphs that have been developed to discuss the reality. Are they up to date, do they have live comments written on them when incidents – abnormalities and non-conformances – have occurred? This is a trigger for making sure people can tell the difference between a problem and an abnormality (or assignable cause of variation, if control charts are being used). If people think that every problem is an abnormality they are almost certainly wrong and will be reacting to all of them, tampering and making things worse. Conversely, if there are no problems but they are not detecting abnormalities then they are losing opportunities to learn.

This is one part of the process manager's job for which data are essential, along with the use of control charts (also known as process behaviour charts) to make sense of it. If there is no data, or it is being interpreted without the informed use of control charts, no one can know if a variation is abnormal (or 'special' or 'assignable'; various terms are used). Thus managers will tend to intervene too often if they think every problem is special, or do nothing if they think all of the variation has a common cause. We strongly advise you to become familiar with the whole subject of statistical process control as soon as possible, and you could bring in anyone in your organisation who has had the training to help you. If there is nobody available, use an external consultant; you will get your money back rapidly.

Maintain workplace organisation

Much of this subject really is common sense, in that people don't need to be convinced of the idea.

> A place for everything, and everything in its place.
> **Mrs Beeton, home economist, 1836–65**

It's not so common in practice, though. Tidiness calls for such a depth of organisational culture and persistence that it is not often maintained over an extended period. The essentials are included in the '5S', workplace organisation discipline.

Sort	Straighten	Shine	Standardise	Sustain
Segregate what is needed, get rid of what is not	Designate a place for everything, and ensure everything is in its place	Clean the workplace and the equipment	Define standards for organising and maintaining the workplace	Employ systems for monitoring the level of achievement

Total Productive Maintenance (TPM)

This is yet another common-sense idea that's not so common. Equipment should be maintained to a standard that means it is always capable of performing to its necessary potential, so that it does not cause loss from breakdown or through gradual wear. Most of us are accustomed to the conditions of a new vehicle guarantee, which requires the owner to have the car serviced at defined intervals by an authorised agent. Modern vehicle systems often detect how the car is used, and issue instructions accordingly on when to have it serviced, based upon the need. However, such discipline is alarmingly rare in many commercial environments where equipment is run until it fails, or buildings are neglected until actual damage occurs as a result of rain coming in.

By applying the principles of understanding the process and its variation, TPM enables operators to predict the maintenance needs and build up a history of economic justification for appropriate changes that are improvements. Don Wheeler's video, 'A Japanese Control Chart' (available on pmi.co.uk), provides an elegant illustration of this approach.

Communicate continually and diligently

As we have previously asserted, if people are to make a meaningful contribution, they need clear goals with which they agree. They also need to know what is going on, both the good and the bad, and they need to feel heard – to consider that their bosses also know what's really happening at the grass roots level. There are two interdependent ways to achieve this:

Broadcasting. This is one-way flow, and is appropriate for information on the big picture, perhaps of company performance or market changes. In all too many cases, it is launched but allowed to lapse, perhaps because the company only spreads good news – except when things are so bad that cutbacks are on the way.

PDSA should be the basis of developing an effective broadcast route. What are you trying to accomplish with it? How will you know if a change is an improvement? People can be asked what they would like to know and in what format. They can be asked what they think of existing information routes.

Although in principle effective broadcasting depends upon a flow from top management, local managers can take the initiative if this flow is absent. A thriving department or operation in the midst of an otherwise dysfunctional organisation is usually characterised by local management having taken the initiative to share what they do know, even in the absence of a company policy. In our experience, this local initiative will generate requests for news about the bigger picture, which should be negotiated with top management.

Two-way Communicating. The word 'communicate' is rooted in the concept of community, of dialogue, sharing and mutual help. The process should always be led by the managers; if they don't do so informal leaders will fill the gap. This has often been the basis of union power.

Many well-established processes can generate two-way communication at work:

- *Team Briefing.* This is a regular, frequent, cascaded conversation between a line boss and their people. Its purpose is to ensure that staff know about the organisation and its performance, and that managers at each level hear about what has been going on in the work. The top-down content is provided by news cascaded from the top management's own team brief, with appropriate additions and subtractions at each level of the hierarchy. The local information is generated at the meetings between line managers and their staff, updating each way, and ensuring mutual understanding.

  The team brief should be part of the discussions at the visual display boards, integrated with other communication and information flows. In this way it reinforces the authority and credibility of local managers. It is easiest when everyone works in one location, but can be successful over the web and teleconferences if the tools are used constructively, and if PDSA is used to refine them.
- *Suggestion schemes.* The purpose of such schemes should be to provide a routine way for staff to make proposals for improvement

or changes that arise from their work. Suggestion schemes have had a bad press over recent decades as a result of having been launched with a high profile only to be abandoned after a few months. The reasons for this failure should be clear to any reader who has made it to this part of the book. Whilst staff members will almost certainly have many ideas to improve the organisation, and be more than willing to submit them, many organisations will probably not be able to adopt them. If processes are not stable, if analytic tools are absent, if the goals are not clear and functions do not cooperate and learn from each other, suggestions will not be successfully implemented and disillusionment will set in.

Worst of all are schemes that escalate suggestions to the top. The pile of proposals in the boss's in-tray speaks volumes about the scope for improvement and the readiness of staff to contribute. But it also confirms the organisation's inability to put the two together and actually make things happen quickly for the better.

But if the organisation has laid the foundations properly, suggestions have naturally flowed at the rate of up to one per month per employee, of which more than ninety-five per cent are implemented. Although this is a bit surprising at first sight – for surely a good organisation hasn't much scope for improvement suggestions – it does actually make sense. No system can ever be perfect, and the situation is changing continually. The best people to notice this are those who see how the work works, and they are most likely to contribute if the culture is right for it. If two-way communication is effective, if local staff and managers have principles and tools to guide their thinking, many suggestions will arise and be implemented locally. If the organisation can learn across its internal and geographic boundaries, then they can be applied more widely and people get wide recognition.

Such communication is a vital aspect of an organisation becoming more self-managing or self-organising. We generally find that staff want to help, but they need to understand goals and progress if they are to be able to contribute with a purpose.

'Listen very carefully, I will say this only twice.'

Electronic communications use redundancy to ensure reliability, and we can learn from that. In fields as variable as transmitting pictures from Saturn, burning a CD or sending an email, a lot more data are sent than seems necessary. This ensures that what was launched was that which was intended, that it got through the noise on the way or that the reader is seeing the message as intended.

What would this mean for managers who wish to communicate more effectively? There are three important steps in the process.

The first is to make sure the message starts out as intended. The digital approach is to insert frequent checks in the coding. Every 'clause' has a validating character that indicates what the clause should say. If the validation does not match the previous content, the machine tries again. The human messenger can do two things to achieve this. The first is to write down the intended message and thus ensure it probably means what they thought; the second is to ask someone else to study its meaning, and modify the text if necessary. Now it's ready to go. A rapid PDSA.

The second step is to differentiate the message from the noise of other messages en route. The digital world chooses frequencies that differ from the background noise. The human communicator needs to be aware of the noise that may obscure their message – for instance, the buzz of endless emails that can swamp the one that counts. If a message about change is important it needs to be sufficiently different to be noticed. Please note, not just with a message flag or a subject line in capital letters!

The third step is to ensure that the recipient has truly heard the message as it was intended. This is not the same as agreeing with it; it's the understanding that's important. In the digital world the reading technology repeats the checks inserted at the writing stage, and if an error is indicated it goes back and tries again using the check figure to change the faulty piece of data. A message about change needs this check too, at the point of receipt. A dialogue is called for between the sender and the receivers, preferably live and frequently. It needs careful design to ensure it is seen as clarification first, even if the recipient does not agree. Unless this loop is completed the sender of the message cannot assume that it has been heard properly. It's another rapid PDSA.

These three principles – 1. validate the correctness of the intended message, 2. ensure it is distinct from the everyday noise and 3. enable the recipient to confirm they have understood – lie at the heart of all good human communication. Following the steps using a learning approach will enable the communicator to develop effective communications for their environment. Whether it is a training workshop, a message about reorganisation or a case study, communication demands time and, yes, redundancy. Anyone can give a speech or send an email with no 'redundant time or resource'; it's quick and easy. But the effects of failure are severe. Each of the three failure modes – of being unclear in the first place, losing the message in the noise of life or of not giving attention to understanding – is enough in itself to undermine the change programme and invalidate its investment.

Redundancy is an emotive word. However in human, as in electronic, communications, it's vital. If you have reached this stage you will recognise some redundancy in this illustration; I have said things more than once. I hope it was enough!

Quality Circles

These are workplace teams focussed upon analysing their work and developing continual improvements. Originally developed in successful Japanese companies, they became very fashionable in the West in the 1980s. Indeed, your author led a very early deployment in administrative offices in 1982 with excellent results. When they are properly supported in a well-structured environment, they can achieve an inspiring combination of tangible improvements, skills enhancement amongst participants and a constructive working atmosphere overall.

Develop skills and knowledge

You and your people need to know *how* to do things as well as what to do. You will have discovered something about existing skill levels during the work in Chapter 1 and now need to build a robust and continuing programme to ensure everyone is able to make their most effective contribution.

The primary purpose of developing skills is to enable everyone to be effective at their work. Learning activities should be mainly focussed on what people need to know, and what they can actually do in their current job. This is a wider focus than just training, with its potential overemphasis on the classroom, or on completing an online curriculum and passing the test. It needs proper preparation for the delegates, and support to them after training in trying things out.

Generalised knowledge. This is the information about the company, its products, processes and policies. All recruits, including temporary ones, need this information. In these days of outsourcing, it can be important that subcontractors who are representing the organisation or who are an integral part of its operations also have this knowledge so that they can act in accordance with the culture of the overall system.

This kind of development should, in large companies, be the responsibility of the HR function, and you should certainly call upon them. If it does not exist it can be developed and tested (PDSA again) on existing staff. In smaller organisations you may have to do it for yourself, but you will not regret the time and energy invested because the consequence is that people are more ready and able to pull together. Health and safety requirements may leave no option but to introduce some induction training if it is absent, but you can use the opportunity to do more than the minimum.

Remember in developing induction training that, apart from whatever the new staff experienced during recruitment, it is their first exposure to how the company works. There is only one chance to make this first impression, so it should not be the poor relation it often seems to be.

Oh, and we have often found that existing staff have been poorly inducted, so they should be the first recipients of such training. Indeed they can be effectively used in both developing and delivering such changes.

Job-related skills. These are the skills necessary to carry out the process or task, such as machine operations, IT packages or techniques such as negotiation or interviewing. There will also be other requirements such as first aid and health and safety. The initial process review will have exposed most of the skill needs.

Process management and improvement skills. These are concerned with understanding how the work works, and how to analyse it so that it can be improved. There are basic levels of competence that you and your people need to develop. Be sure, as leader, to learn first and be seen to practise, and you thus set an example to the rest of your team. Change demands leadership as well as management; you need to be the one to decide what is appropriate for your people, and this knowledge can only come from your practice.

Monitoring personal performance

In large organisations managers are required to participate in some kind of performance management system, as both assessors of their own staff and in being assessed themselves. In many cases such appraisals provide the legitimate basis of training and development planning, which can be positive. In some cases assessments or appraisals are linked to pay, which can have a negative impact on general motivation. Combining appraisals for potential and development with assessment of performance for salary usually undermines both.

As with all other work, (and the hint lies strongly in the name performance management 'system'), it needs to be seen as a process with a purpose, and an explicit flow. It also needs to be understood in relation to its wider system. Furthermore, PDSA should be applied to the process on the basis of evidence.

We are sceptical about the theory behind using such formal systems to distribute salary increases or bonuses. Our experience is that the overwhelming majority of people wish to do a good job for their employer or customer. If leaders do their job, as described in this book, their people will want to make the work work properly. Being able to make a difference to your working conditions appeals to your intrinsic motivation and is much more effective and enduring than receiving monetary rewards in response to the achievement of a target. The fact that such targets are usually in themselves arbitrary and actually not within the complete control of the person being assessed only adds to the potential disillusionment. A few individuals get some kind of reward whereas many who have done a decent job get nothing.

What is called for is leadership from line managers. This means engaging staff in the goals of the organisation, tackling the barriers in the way and recognising their contributions. People are individuals, with widely differing needs and wants, responses to their workplace, family environments and so on. This means that leaders have a never-ending job to try and understand the individuals and respond accordingly to each. This is, of course, time consuming and often difficult, but rewards all parties when done well. Setting targets, appraising people, categorising them and rewarding by formulae do not equal leadership – and do not encourage them to contribute their best.

We recognise that it can be very hard to go against the grain of an organisation's payment system. Forty years ago a manager could go for years without a proper review meeting with their boss, performance management systems were rare, and a few headline examples seemed to work for a while. Now they are everywhere. They seem to gather a vast bureaucracy of HR functions and specialist contractors, and almost have a life of their own in spite of there being little evidence that they motivate people and help them to achieve more ambitious targets.

We suggest that you attempt to understand the performance management system in your own organisation by using process management concepts and tools, and engage in dialogue with leaders to apply them in the least bad way. Some parts – such as routine skills appraisal and development planning – are needed, but using them to rank people would be best given up, just like smoking. If you work on the principle that most people would like to do their best for their employer and help them to do so in a structured way, you will often be rewarded.

Your own approach to leading

All the above methods require coaching and collaborative behaviours by the senior managers. They involve asking questions about how things are organised, what the data reveal, and using PDSA to share theories and jointly assess their validity and to keep away from personality-based enquiries.

Our experience is that this is much the best way to get the best contributions from all staff. At heart, most people want to do a good job and to contribute to improving their place of work.

However, this is not to advocate a detached, impersonal approach. Leadership is about carrying people with you in spirit, exciting them about the value of what they are doing and not seeing them just as process operators going through the motions. Your sense of humour, empathy and optimism are just as important in a process-based world as in the hierarchical world of old. Be aware that your mood sets the mood of the department, so how you hold yourself as you go through the day is important. If you look subdued and tentative for whatever reason your people will most likely interpret this as something to do with the prospects for their jobs.

You need help to develop these behaviours. It can be very valuable for you to find a third party with whom to share your doubts about your work; there are sure to be some. We explore some possibilities for this in Chapter 10.

Process management maturity

You can make a rough assessment of progress by revisiting the matrix introduced in Chapter 1 and comparing your comments. You have learned a lot, so don't be surprised if you change your mind about what you recorded earlier, but don't lose those comments; such a comparison is valuable when you are talking with others.

Level	Meaning	Comments at time of first study	Comments after establishing process management
1	The key processes are identified.		
2	Ownership of them has been established, and their purpose is understood.		
3	They are formally flowcharted / documented and standardised operations can be seen.		
4	Appropriate and visible measures are used to monitor the processes and enable learning.		
5	Feedback from customers, suppliers and other processes is sought and used as the basis for improvement.		
6	An improvement and review mechanism is in place with targets for improvement.		
7	Processes are systematically managed for continual improvement, and learning is shared.		
8	The processes are benchmarked against best practice.		
9	The processes are regularly challenged and re-engineered if required.		
10	The processes are a role model for other organisations.		

Ann brought the drinks to the table, and put them down in front of her two friends, rather too hard. She needed some sympathetic ears away from work. After a few weeks of consolidation in making her work work more predictably she was seeing that some degree of stability was both achievable and useful, although it took a lot of effort and there was a lot more to do. But she knew that wouldn't hold their attention for long. It was a rule she had apparently broken, and how her boss had reacted, that she needed to let off steam about.

A few days after helping her manager to get the bank off his back, she had spoken to her boss when he got back from holiday. Far from being supportive, he had been highly critical of her breaking protocols, committing the company to support a bad loan (which she hadn't done), interfering, all kinds of sins. She should have taken no action without reference to HR, and he was not interested in any reasons; them not being there either was no excuse, regardless of the urgency. Ann felt threatened and let down; the sweepstake letter was on her mind again.

Her friends were great. They would have done the same, they said, and were sure it would blow over. But it was a sobering reminder of the perils of taking risks, even with the best possible motivation, and also of the balance to be struck between following rules to the letter and using one's initiative when necessary. She would need to find a way to get that across to her people, though she would not be able to use this particular illustration!

On the train home she felt a little better, and both of her friends had envied the freedom of action she had created in her new job. She looked over her notes for the last few weeks on maintaining performance.

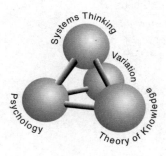

Systems thinking:

- They had made some process changes in advance of their being needed, thanks to sales letting them know of a new campaign. In turn this better information had arisen because of new relationships made during the first project.
- Now she had a better feeling for how her whole function worked she felt ready to accept an invitation to visit a partner company in Europe.

Variation:

- The workplace displays had mostly been well received, but they had not been properly absorbed. Some weren't up to date when she visited; some were not understood by the people working right next to them. Yet another training need.
- The graphs on most of the displays were better than nothing, but few people could interpret them well. She had been on an SPC awareness course and needed to go on a longer programme; every time she learnt something it seemed to expose her ignorance and that wasn't comfortable.

Theory of knowledge:

- Here was one really positive aspect, conversations were becoming richer. A few people were talking about theories and evidence, wanting to test before jumping into action. She had to make sure the others did too.

Psychology:

- She wondered how long it would take to feel that people trusted her. She had tried to be consistent, and tried to listen properly. She felt she had to accept that a boss could never be completely trusted and she could never give the reassurances people craved. A site might be closed, technology might move on, the company could fail. So she could only set an example when it was within her power to do so. She would try – and surely she would try harder than her own boss?
- She had attended a conference and heard a presentation about Quality Circles, and the presenter had been really quite enthusiastic when she found him after the talk. They had experienced a surge of

enthusiasm, as to be expected at first, but it had carried on for over a year afterwards. She had also been asked to make a presentation about her work, but thought it too early just yet.

- Her principal concern was the persistent use of targets and bonuses for achieving throughput and shortening telephone calls. It had been this way for so many years, and no matter that the consequences had often been chaotic after the fuss had died down. It meant that several of the supervisors tended to shout and cheer, take short cuts and drive staff on when the pressure mounted. She would simply have to stay calm, persist and demonstrate the value of effective processes focussed on the customer. It just didn't sound very exciting.

7 Dealing with problems

If I had an hour to solve a problem I'd spend fifty-five minutes thinking about the problem and five minutes thinking about solutions.

Albert Einstein, theoretical physicist, 1879–1955

Ann's story

Two months later, and this next meeting didn't feel like it was going to be fun in anyone's definition of the term. It was 8.00 in the morning, the chairman's office had been on the phone late yesterday afternoon because a furious customer had escalated a complaint about a mishandled cheque. Every possible party seemed to have piled into the issue at the end of the day: her boss, the press office again, there was even talk of the regulator being involved. The sweepstake letter came back to her mind.

Ann was glad now of the trouble she had taken to communicate the steps taken so far, but of course her audience hadn't included the chairman. His secretary had passed on a message in which he had apparently muttered that this new customer service manager should 'get a grip'.

So she had convened this meeting as soon as it could be held, with a couple of managers on the teleconference speaker. There was so much history that there was little energy to do much more than smooth things over and get on with the work, no matter what the consequences were. But she was determined to stick with her process approach, and really there wasn't any alternative except for the old one of looking for someone to blame. It wouldn't be easy, asking methodical questions about the work and not just demanding to know who had done what in order to find a scapegoat. They needed a plan of informed action, and it had to be made clear over the next hour that a methodical approach was not a soft option to delay decisions, but that it was the demanding option that would lead to improvement, and that she was determined to use it.

Not making a drama out of a crisis

No matter how secure your processes, surprises happen and some of them will adversely impact the customer. But you can use surprises constructively. Organisations that solve problems in ways that reduce the chance of repetition become ever more predictable. They are also likely to be better at dealing with surprises when something nearly goes wrong. Possibly the best example of learning from problems is the civil airline industry, where for generations there have been both rigorous independent investigations into disasters and a no-fault culture of reporting near misses, those incidents that threaten safety. Taken in combination this has ensured that mistakes are very rarely repeated. This is not the case in most environments we have encountered, where blame and threat combine to keep near misses undeclared and accidents are brushed off wherever possible, but with prosecution lurking for those unfortunate to be around when things really fail. Any system that includes the threat of prosecution is unlikely to learn much from its mistakes.

The context for 'problem-driven improvement' is that of the Process Management Cycle introduced in Chapter 5 with Standardise, and discussed in Chapter 6: 'Maintain'. Here we complete the explanation with 'Improve'.

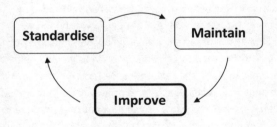

> *For want of a nail the shoe was lost;*
> *For want of a shoe the horse was lost;*
> *For want of a horse the battle was lost;*
> *For the failure of battle the kingdom was lost –*
> *All for the want of a horseshoe nail.*
> **Anon; original is thirteenth-century German**

When a crisis strikes it can be hard to keep your sense of proportion as the pressure mounts. However, you will find that the experience of what you have so far achieved will provide a foundation. When you combine the logic of PDSA together with the behaviours of increasing readiness to change you can do a much better job of getting the problem resolved, and uncovering the systemic issues that lay behind it. And, as the ancient rhyme makes clear, there are always systemic issues. Very few problems emerge from nowhere; they are the tips of an iceberg of causal factors that have remained hidden until some unfortunate combination of circumstances came together.

The first step is to get everyone to the same state of awareness.

What is the context of variation that led to the problem?
When faced with an urgent problem you will find that a variation context diagram such as this will help the team place the issue in the system, and guide you on deciding who should be involved with the urgent work. A key point here is to ask questions based upon variation, not just on the failure incident itself.

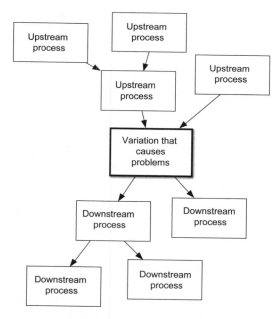

Variation context diagram

You will probably need to facilitate the group carefully to think in process and variation terms. Most people volunteer information about outputs, inputs, people, companies, departments – in fact, almost anything but process – in their first answers. The diagram forces them into process language, and language affects how people think. If they are all to understand the ups and downs of the flow of activities they have to use the language of process, expressing verb–noun, and sticking with this may take some persistence when the pressure is on. Some examples include 'maintain equipment' rather than 'maintenance', or 'select suppliers' rather than 'purchasing'.

Asking about variation increases the evidence that will emerge: there will be plenty of history in the near misses but perhaps very few previous failures. A loose nail in a horse's hoof may not be a problem right now, but it indicates one that was about to happen.

Deal with immediate needs *and* get to the bottom of the process

All problems are outcomes of a process or combination of processes. As suggested above, the only way to reduce or eliminate the chance of recurrence is to understand and improve the processes. However, this is likely to take time, and time is usually short when there is a customer complaint, an injured person or a chemical leak.

Someone may therefore need to be dispatched to provide immediate assistance at the place of the incident whilst the enquiry is getting going, perhaps before you are sure what happened, never mind why it happened. There's no need for them to be defensive about not knowing causes, however; they should just make it clear that you have a structure to get to the roots of the problem to prevent its recurrence. Get someone as senior as possible on the road immediately after the first meeting, especially with serious incidents. Many organisations' reputations are based upon how they respond to problems rather than how they deliver everyday results, and problems are an opportunity to be different in the eyes of the customer. Being really proactive provides opportunities to delight even in the toughest of circumstances.

This 'problem-driven improvement' flowchart provides the disciplined questions needed to deal with the immediate consequences and generate learning (other useful approaches are also available, including the 8D methodology). What is important is to keep to PDSA, and require the team to be prepared to work intensively to spin the cycle several times during the activity. Even if only a few hours are available, you must persist with the use of PDSA; shortcuts risk failure at some later stage. There are likely to be some strong views about 'this' leading to 'that', and multiple tests may be needed. Just because a variation correlates with an outcome does not mean it necessarily caused it.

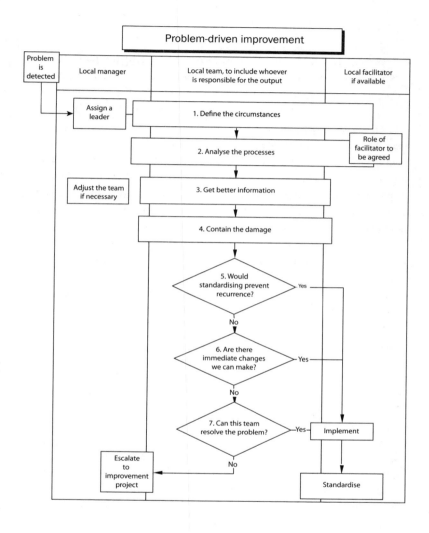

Each stage has some powerful questions:

 1. *Define the circumstances.* What actually happened, or seemed to happen? This means asking the customer, probably visiting the part of the process in which the problem became evident and any other area that seems immediately relevant. The term 'customer' will need to be broad in this case, as the problem may have caused an accident or damage, or perhaps a financial loss to people who have no contractual relationship to the organisation. There is no substitute for getting to the people affected, no matter how angry and unpleasant may be the prospect of the encounter. Such anger amongst people experiencing failures is made much worse if they feel they are being ignored, so here is an immediate opportunity to defuse it.

Consider the communication (two-way if at all possible, see Chapter 6) you need to make, and with stakeholders as well as customers. You are probably using a different approach in dealing with the problem to the established pattern, so that will need explaining at various stages. You are seeking support for the forthcoming actions, and to influence others by your example.

2. Analyse the processes

> I keep six honest serving-men (They taught me all I knew);
> their names are What and Why and When and How and
> Where and Who.
> **Rudyard Kipling, British writer, 1865–1936**

 Use the information from step 1 above to analyse the process, possibly also the upstream and downstream associated processes, taking care to gather comments from operators, and no matter if they don't appear directly relevant. What was varying, when did the problem happen, when did it not happen? Has it happened, or nearly happened, before? Is measurement reliability an issue, could it have happened but not been detected? Study any documentation carefully; are the standards easy to follow, are they doable?

 3. *Get better information.*
Based upon this analysis there will almost certainly be gaps in the information or data that are produced, so these will have to be obtained urgently.

4. Contain the damage.

Throughout the first three steps look to identify where and how you could ensure no repetition of the incident. Look also to resolve the issue with the customer, in terms of replacement or compensation. You may find that customers tend to be less aggressive once they see that you are taking their complaint seriously, and may indeed provide extra information.

Revisit the communication you have done so far, and take steps to ensure that stakeholders you worked with in step 2 are up to date with your progress, as well as others who may have emerged.

5. Would standardising eliminate recurrence?

Generate some theories. (This could be done in parallel with step 4.) Did the problem arise because the process was not followed? If so, test whether following the process would eliminate repetition. If this is the case, take steps to ensure process compliance in future. These steps may include training and information provision, and not necessarily disciplinary measures. Short cuts may have been made in such things as maintenance schedules or the quality of materials being bought.

Ask 'why?' five times to get beyond the obvious symptoms.

6. Are there immediate changes we can make?

Make them. If the process was being followed and the trouble happened, you have a serious case of an incapable process. Its natural variation can lead to non-conformances. The first step is, as always in this problem response context, to put a fix in place to protect the customer, in this case for the foreseeable future.

It may be possible to make process changes that will make it capable, but they need proper testing through PDSA. It's thus likely that an improvement project will be needed, as described in Chapter 8. The communication you have previously done will pay dividends at this stage, as potential participants should already be aware and wanting to help.

7. Can this team resolve the problem?

Is the scale of the likely project suitable for the skills,

capabilities and time of the team that has been doing this investigation? If it is, you can proceed to develop a project charter with them and sponsor the improvement activity. If, as is more likely, the scope is beyond this particular team, you will need to keep customer protection in place whilst a separate project is organised.

Review the activity

When the problem has been resolved use PDSA with the team, and stakeholders if possible, to understand how the resolution process worked and to help run it better next time. For there is always a next time.

Note also the obsession with process throughout. Whilst it is possible that an individual wilfully ignored instructions, took a shortcut or just got distracted, these occasions are most unlikely to be the real issue. Even where it looks like an individual's 'fault' there is nearly always a systemic cause, be it in recruitment, induction, training, technology, communication: the list of possibilities is endless. Disciplining people can keep bosses quiet, but it won't lead to better processes in future.

Over the years there have been miscarriages of justice by authorities prosecuting individuals for 'causing' problems while it turned out that their behaviour was, in fact, routine, a consequence of incapability in the process. A recent example in the UK was a train guard who gave permission for the driver to start even though an intoxicated person was leaning against the train and was killed. The guard was jailed for neglect of duty, while in fact it turned out that he could not see clearly because of the position of the switch in the carriage. When the other guards were instructed to follow the rules to the letter the whole process was slowed so much that the timetable could not be maintained. But there was no appeal; the guard still served a prison sentence, and one can easily imagine the resentment of the other guards about the lack of support from their employer.

Fear will not lead to the openness that is a prerequisite for learning.

If there don't seem to be any problems, that could be a problem

No news is not necessarily good news. If no surprises emerge over an extended time in daily operations there will be no learning. Problems can take many forms, ranging from letting the customer down to overproviding resources and hence costing too much, or non-conformances that escape being noticed in spite of best efforts in process monitoring. These are the trees that are still falling over but nobody seems to be there when it happens.

Problems are being hidden

Maybe customers are not complaining, just moving away or simply couldn't care. Maybe they are complaining, but issues are being dealt with and no records kept.

The task is too easy for the process

If the work works really well – in other words, if it is effective and adaptable – maybe it needs looking at to see how it can be made more efficient. You need to be constantly on the lookout for opportunities to match your resources with the needs of generating the output in accordance with what you know of customer needs. If you don't put pressure on to improve productivity in this rational way, sooner or later you will be pressured to do so against some kind of arbitrary target. A Quality Circle activity, as briefly described in Chapter 6, is a good way of engaging the staff in improving how their work works even when it seems to be doing well enough.

The process is OK now, but may not be at some future (predictable) time

Many factors can disrupt routine and they don't have to be a surprise. Depending upon the organisation and its environment, workloads vary during the year. Holidays, festivals, sports events, epidemics, the weather – the list is long. You will build a picture of many of these as your first year in a job progresses, but meanwhile you should conduct a working session with your team to list the ones they have experienced, and carry out a contingency analysis on them, as described in Chapter 3. The eight wastes described in Chapter 1 are another way to uncover opportunities.

For instance, in the travel business it's worth knowing the local holiday and sports calendars for the various destinations you deal with; there's no point providing discounted seats when there's a tournament scheduled. In the food industry it's usual for the period between Christmas and New Year to be one of the busiest times, and your department's holidays may need to be rationed. On the other hand that time is likely to be inactive in recruitment services, so holidays should be taken then.

You will also find much to ponder in reports and TV programmes on disasters such as oil rig blowouts, shipwrecks, plane crashes and so on. Look for the issues in process terms and you will find some sobering connections with your work; problems noticed but not learned from.

This is moving on from problem solving to problem prevention, and once the attitudes and behaviours are established you will find it is never-ending; there's no chance you will run out of possible problems to anticipate! It expands on the need for a process to be adaptable, as well as effective and efficient as discussed in Chapter 2.

Much will be known about such variation in your department or in the support parts of the organisation such as HR, finance or sales. However, in our experience such knowledge is not systematically collected and shared, and each manager builds up an informal picture over the years. When they move on the newcomer has to start from scratch. A common reason we find for clients not wanting to write up a case study is because, after the presentation of the results of a project someone says 'ah, we knew that five years ago, we stopped doing XXX or YYY after last year's budget cut'. They don't want such embarrassment to be made public.

Of course you mustn't become too obsessive and reactive. You are seeking evidence that will help to make process changes, not to get into the habit of immediate reaction to the ups and downs of everyday variation. Some days will always be better than others.

Share your learning with stakeholders

Every problem will have a natural population of stakeholders who are directly affected or just (just!) interested in it. Some of them will no doubt be closely involved with the resolution efforts outlined in the problem-driven improvement work, but others may only be vaguely aware of what has happened.

You should take this opportunity to keep stakeholders informed and reassured that not only has the problem been fixed, but that the team followed a discipline to ensure it is not repeated. In most organisations there are so many problems that people cannot keep track of those they are not directly involved with. They may hear about an incident being resolved, but probably wouldn't be surprised if it occurs again. If it really does not repeat they will probably have forgotten about it and won't think to credit any particular approach for the improvement.

We are reluctant to use the cliché of every problem being an opportunity, but if you are prepared to use PDSA within the discipline of the problem-driven improvement approach, and to Study its use each time a problem appears, you will find it's true. It reinforces all of the process management work you have done so far, and demonstrates that PDSA is certainly better than the traditional RFA (Ready, Fire, Aim) or DDDF (Do, Do, Do, Firefight) that is so common.

Ann's reflections

The last few days had been quite a test, Ann thought, and in her own mind she felt she had passed. Somehow she had stayed calm; the process had helped every step of the way. Better than that, when she called the press office manager to let him know how things had worked out, it turned out he had also somehow heard of the issue with the mortgage loan. 'Well done,' he said, 'just what I would have done.' 'Thanks very much indeed,' she replied, perhaps a little too enthusiastically, 'I got a hard time over that from my boss.' He had not been surprised at that, told her not to worry and to stick with her attitude of trusting her own judgement. So no worries about the sweepstake after all, she thought.

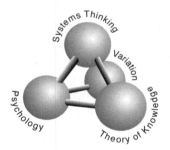

She had fresh appetite for her notes; maybe the time for the conference speech was getting closer?

Systems thinking:

- Everyone had learned a lot about the whole process, and not just the flash point, as a result of having to take the overview.
- There was still a mystery about how the procedures had been allowed to get into the state where the error could happen, not be noticed, and then get lost again when the first complaint emerged. Too many

people had been partially involved a couple of years before. No one was prepared to be definitive; transparency was too risky, apparently.

Variation:

- The problem really did seem to be a surprise – in the sense that a lot of things had to go wrong for it to happen – so it had not led to any particular changes being appropriate. Ann felt that if they had been monitoring all the processes involved it would have been caught before it escalated, but couldn't be sure about it. It would have to wait until more people were trained and they had been monitoring for many months.
- What had become clear was that the IT process design team had taken no account at all for variation reduction or even monitoring at the design stage. That would need to change, but she was now convinced it would get support on the next such project.

Theory of knowledge:

- Language had been a problem right from the start of the investigations. Not foreign language, but disciplined use of English: confusions over 'days' (calendar days or working days?), authority levels for signing claims, references to job roles and even departments. Paperwork could be contradictory and personal opinions as to what was good enough varied frighteningly. There was plenty of scope for future improvement through clarity and plain writing (just like my notes, she thought).

Psychology:

- There were a few 'ah-has' in the team as they followed the process. It had seemed so obvious at various stages, even if the questions had never been asked before. In spite of some frustrations at the initial delay whilst they looked into the details, everyone had joined in the enthusiasm at the review. A lot of them said they would use the flowchart. Ann wondered, though, how many would still take shortcuts.

8 Improving on a larger scale

The reasonable man adapts himself to the world. The unreasonable man persists in trying to adapt the world to himself. Therefore, all progress depends on the unreasonable man.
George Bernard Shaw, writer, 1856–1950

Ann's story

This was more like it, another meeting to prepare for, but not a crisis this time – in fact, it seemed to have arisen as a result of her response to the flap over the complaint to the chairman's office. Their work had shown that the problem had been an old one, one that had surfaced months before she arrived, and which had been waiting on a decision in finance: nothing to do with her time in the department. But, whatever the details, Ann had persisted with the problem-driven improvement process in tackling it and many questions had needed to be answered. This had eventually led to both the finance head and the boss of the press office realising that they had gaps in their processes, and somehow – perhaps because of her newness in the job – they had not been quite as defensive as she expected, or maybe it was the logic of the problem-solving process itself. Whatever the reason, they had commented that she seemed to be bringing something new. She felt she could scrap the sweepstake letter at last but was keeping it – it could be fun at the Christmas party.

Her boss had then asked her to join him with his peers to consider what should be the change priorities for the next year in the whole sales and marketing function. He had been more supportive of late though he made no further reference to the mortgage incident; was this good or bad?

Anyway, the meeting would give her the chance to lobby to do a proper job on the compensation issue. What they had done so far was just a reprieve, really. They still had to check far too many documents, and there was something odd about the way that some weeks would produce no problems whilst others would have several. She was reasonably confident that very few cheques were getting through to customers without explanation, but slightly less confident that any complaint a customer did need to make would be well handled. She was really sure it was all costing too much. She thought that it all deserved more attention but the scale of the project required to deal with it was beyond her authority, and she couldn't be sure of the timescale or the likely changes needed to automate the solution.

She turned again to the charts with the data of incidents, she needed to be sure she understood the story they told.

Leading larger scale change (multiple PDSAs)

The work so far has been learning about and improving the work within a department manager's responsibility, getting the show on the road and keeping it there. It is on the left hand and middle parts of this model.

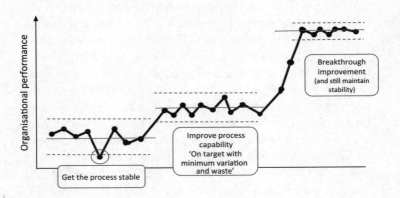

As you become more practised in using the process management approach you will be aware of how much better could be the performance of the work if you could look beyond your department's horizons. You will probably become progressively more dissatisfied with how the work is done wherever you look, not just in your department or even in your own organisation. From supermarket queues to insurance claims, airline booking problems or computer faults, you will find yourself becoming irritated with things being so inconsistent and often inadequate. You might find that you have to hold yourself back from making comments about service in the presence of friends and family, who will perhaps regard you as a bit obsessed. Maybe they are right. Mine have had to get used to it!

However, on the good side, this questioning attitude is great for leading strategic change and improvement projects, which are an essential part of any manager's career development. If you are prepared to be unreasonable, like George Bernard Shaw, but in a constructive manner, you will be able to make a real difference.

Anyone who has applied the process management principles of Chapters 1 to 7 is therefore well prepared to take on the second of the three management roles shown in the diagram below – leading a demanding project to redevelop a major cross-functional process in order to achieve a step change in its performance. This practical experience of leading a large-scale project is priceless if you are later asked to act as sponsor to one, a key role for top managers. The System of Profound Knowledge applies and PDSA must form the basis of understanding the current situation, and developing and testing theories. Any of the tools so far used will also prove relevant, whilst new tools learned in larger scale projects will be found to have application in the everyday work.

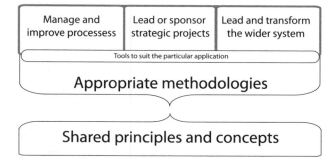

Large-scale improvement work does of course need some additional methodologies and disciplines in deciding what to work on, how the project work should work, and how its progress will be reviewed.

Which major projects?

Major improvement projects may emerge from the regular work, or be deployed from the top. Senior management must lead the prioritisation work as there are always too many candidates and never enough resources to improve everything. Projects need to be focussed on objectives that senior management consider important and thus worth the undoubted trouble. In addition, since the implementation of any major project is likely to be time consuming for line managers, a degree of realism from the top is needed to avoid swamping them with too many changes at once.

Three aspects of the organisation generate candidates for major projects:

1. Candidates emerging from the daily work

As we have seen in Chapters 6 and 7, you can use the Process Management Cycle and the problem-driven improvement approach to deal with issues as they arise, whilst recognising that some issues are too demanding to be handled within the function and need escalating. This will depend upon many factors including the scale of the organisation, the resources and skills available, and the urgency and importance of the issue. You may need to accumulate a number of candidates during the year in order to discuss priorities at the annual planning meetings. Some may emerge with urgency and require reprioritisation. Beware of becoming too focused on sticking with an annual plan, no matter what changes.

2. Local policies and priorities

Your peer group will also be reviewing its experience of everyday operations, and hopefully engaging with the each other on the market, customers, suppliers and stakeholders (and so on) in order to assess future needs. All this information needs to be synthesised into a high-level priority list, and a few major projects agreed.

3. Top management or group priorities

The board of directors or equivalent governing body should continually revisit the strategic prospects for the organisation, and in Chapter 9 we explore some of the insights provided by the process management approach. Their decisions will generate needs for change or improvement work that involves large parts of the organisation – and possibly outsiders too, such as suppliers.

Agreeing the overall balance of projects

These three categories of projects need to be brought together to form a complete list of candidates. The top management team has to decide which ones are to be given a high profile and support, and which are left to the local management to conduct within their own resources.

Coordinating multiple priorities

Why the number of major improvement projects must be small
There must only be a few major cross-functional projects, certainly in single figures and perhaps initially only two or three. We have no illusions that it is easy to stick with this limit, but are also convinced of the need for determination to concentrate the efforts, for several reasons:

- Leading a major cross-functional project is difficult, perhaps the toughest challenge any leader will face until they reach the board. This will not surprise the reader of this book, as the difficulties of increasing readiness to change are hard enough for a line boss within their own department. These difficulties are harder still for project leaders who will not have executive authority to apply across the functions. Important projects therefore need the best people to be leading them, probably full time, and that is hard for the organisation to arrange.
- The skills needed to lead or facilitate major improvement projects are usually new, and it takes time and practice to develop the necessary confidence.
- Major projects need confident sponsorship from top management. There needs to be a top manager who is ready, willing and able to sponsor each major project. Sponsorship is a non-executive role that supports the leader, provides a connection for the team to the top management and is prepared to deal with top management politics. Projects that do not get this commitment must be postponed or given a lower profile because they will not achieve their goal in the absence of proper sponsorship.
- Major projects demand the time and effort of everyday managers and many others in cooperating with the learning and implementation

work, and perhaps in changing their own behaviour. Implementing multiple changes often disappoints through conflict of interest, time and priorities across departments.

- As well as a highly competent leader, major projects require confident, experienced facilitation from people who have in-depth knowledge of the principles, methodologies and tools. Ideally, these facilitators are internal people, but they must be potential high flyers and will take many months to develop the basic skills, hence limiting the scale of what can be achieved. Alternatively they may be external people, but top quality ones are in short supply. Recruiting outsiders as facilitators can seem an economical option, but you need to take great care that they have the wide experience and interpersonal skills needed to be able to adjust rapidly to their new environment – and their qualification level may not be a good indication of that.

Major projects are not likely to be suitable for those undergoing training to practise upon. In order to support learning they need to be limited in scope, and focussed on the use of the methods rather than the delivery of the results. Many change programmes have compromised this purpose by launching multiple high-profile projects, with the result that most of the trainees are under too much pressure to deliver and the projects founder.

This is all likely to be depressing as it seems to limit ambition, but we are sure that experienced readers will agree with it. We have seen presentations of programmes where a large number of projects seemed to be generating good results, but in every case that we investigated the story was not so clear in reality. Some projects had achieved much, but the rest were in truth falling well short of the claims. Whilst public talks get good initial publicity, unfortunately it's often the failures that get the attention over the longer term and give the approach its reputation.

Taking these factors into account, keeping to a small number of major projects that are well run and supported – and which deliver their goals – is a powerful way of building foundations for long-term change and continuing transformation.

Large scale projects as vehicles for organisational transformation

We discussed the dream of the Four Es in Chapter 1: 'The organisation is achieving its goals, and can demonstrate its management and improvement approach Everywhere, Everyday, by Everyone, for Ever.'

This table indicates how large-scale projects contribute to this ambition.

Characteristic	Contribution of major projects
Everywhere. Across the whole organisation, including strategy development, everyday work and projects.	By being multifunction, with strategic goals, and implemented into everyday processes.
Everyday. Leaders understand and can explain the relationship between how they approach their work and the overall improved results they have achieved.	In order for the changes to be permanent, leaders have had to make links between methods behind the achievements of the projects and their implementation into daily management.
By **Everyone.** The approach is used in depth where appropriate, and can be explained by line managers and staff routinely, and not just by the improvement personnel.	Active sponsorship by top management ensures they understand that the approach is different. Continual review of the improvement process means that all involved have helped adapt the approach and don't have to rely on specialists.
For **Ever.** It has clearly been applied and developed over many years.	As the large-scale projects take root and the approach is used again and again, participation becomes part of everyone's career development.

Leading improving projects

We make no excuses here for repeating the 'hamburger model' first referred to in Chapter 3. One of your tasks in leading a project is to increase readiness to change in both the team members and those around the work in order to minimise the chances of socio-emotional issues derailing it.

This requires attention to the same issues described in Chapter 3 as being relevant to the problem-solving work, but on a broader scale.

Establishing the team and the charter

The terms of reference of the project need first to be established between the sponsor and the team leader, and should include at least the following:

- A clear purpose, one clearly linked to performance benefits for the customer if at all possible.
- A list of benefits and of specific deliverables as far as can be understood at this stage.
- A list of team members, and the degree of their commitment.
- An estimated timescale.
- The scope of the project across the organisation.
- Enablers that will help the project succeed.
- Barriers which may get in the way if not addressed.

This first charter then needs to be worked through by the team. Many of these factors will almost certainly need to be refined by dialogue with the sponsor as the project moves forwards and the knowledge develops.

Improvement project structure

PMI's Improvement Cycle is built on many decades of practical experience. It expands upon the Six Sigma DMAIC problem-solving model, and balances the need for individual steps that are seen as achievable with a

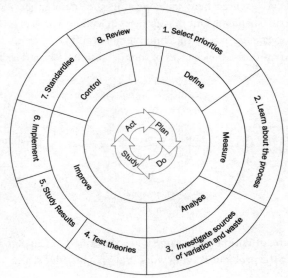

visible overview of the tasks being undertaken. It can be applied to small- and large-scale projects with equal levels of usefulness and rigour and can easily be adapted to innovation as to improvement.

Its power comes from its coherent structure and its strong relationship with the PDSA Cycle. It can be applied to all types of projects and time frames, not only problem-solving projects. The PDSA Cycle should be spinning many times, helping to develop and adapt theories within each of eight stages. It also generates learning about projects in general and this in turn provides a consistent approach that encourages people to share learning about the methodology across many projects.

Throughout the project you must ensure that meetings are properly run, and will of course find that the meeting management processes you have used so far are valuable here too.

1. Select Priorities emphasises the importance of creating a firm foundation for starting the project. It should be launched with a charter, as described above, which ensures that you are tackling the issues in a way that maximises the chance of success. These are of course unlikely to be obvious. The team must repeatedly ask 'What are we trying to accomplish?' and 'How will we know that a change is an improvement?'. If the whole team is engaged in this process, then the common understanding of purpose pays dividends as the project moves forward. During this phase, the team and the senior management sponsor should engage in dialogue to convert the initial deliverables of the project into logical goals with time scales based on knowledge. This should be formalised into a contract.

The leader and facilitator must beware at this stage of being driven into solutions and implementation before the causal chain has been understood. The pressure from top management may be extreme and the urgency apparent in the style of reviews with the sponsor. Hence the need for strong characters in both sponsor and leader roles. They should have had experience at a smaller scale if not previously on such a high-profile project. There is no point using a sophisticated learning structure, intended to uncover new knowledge, if the leadership thinks it knows the answer and is determined to force a solution. A dialogue that avoids wasted effort in further investigation will in this case be called for. You may be somewhat discouraged to read this in step 1 of an 8-step model, but we do counsel such honesty now as being a lot less painful in the long run. Skilled coaching of both sponsor and leader will pay dividends.

2. Learn about the process challenges the current organisational view of what is happening. You already know that the reality of the workplace often diverges hugely from theories that may be strongly held, so it is extremely important for the team to understand the processes as they actually operate. To be certain of this understanding, they should listen to and observe the stakeholder groups involved with the processes. This will reveal what is really going on and begin the process of engaging others in the whole improvement process. At this stage you may uncover some disconcerting assumptions that need careful handling.

This phase is concluded, as are the others, by a review with the sponsor. It may surprise them, for most top managers hope that all is running as it says in the book with some details to be adjusted. When this is clearly not so it can undermine their confidence: they hoped the project would be about improving, not having to reconsider fundamental principles.

There may be some immediate and obvious changes to make, as discussed in Chapter 2. These need to be attended to or the whole project may be compromised, and your earlier experience will pay dividends here too. The team will learn more than it expects about getting agreement over supposedly small and simple changes, and this will be a useful rehearsal for later, wider-scale implementation.

3. Investigate sources of variation and waste brings together the acknowledgement that all processes vary both in themselves and through their interdependencies as they operate within the wider system. Understanding these variations provides a means for assessing their effect on the outputs for customers. The team needs to understand the impact of the cause and effect relationships between different processes within the system to develop theories of waste and variation at the systemic level. These theories need to be verified with data, and rigorous statistical methods are essential.

Much of this, of course, has become routine for you if you have been applying the lessons from earlier on, but is none the less powerful for that. If you have not so far become familiar with statistical process control, make sure you have experienced practitioners available to help. It's still not too late to start learning it yourself, but the complexities of most projects demand in-depth experience in statistical analysis.

4. Test Theories. Theories for solutions to address root causes should be generated and evaluated through PDSA, in a safe way that allows them to be modified or withdrawn without too much cost if the theory proves not to work effectively. Multiple tests may be required. Testing should not lead to an all or nothing decision to accept or reject. Instead, the tests build information and knowledge about both the theory and the system within which it has been tested. It may be appropriate to test theories to disprove them, rather than just looking for positive evidence.

5. Study Results stresses the importance of understanding the results and implications of the tests as opposed to simply reacting to them. There needs to be a period of reflection during which people can extract learning that may remain dormant unless it is developed proactively. Why was the idea that was evaluated new, when it probably seems obvious now? Or, perhaps worse, why have we evaluated something we thought was new that worked, but which actually turned out to be something we used to do but has been allowed to lapse?

This is also the stage at which you can help people to draw on the systemic perspective to understand not only the direct cause and effect relationships found in the data but also to look for any by-products of new knowledge which may help towards new approaches to solving other process problems. This demands that people generalise the principles of what was achieved, so that others in different processes may be able to relate to it. Such matters as communications, honest data, customer-focused measures, are all universal issues but may not appear relevant to others if not generalised.

If the study shows the solutions were not valid the team needs to go back to investigating sources of variation and waste once more. The better the team worked on looking for disconfirming evidence at the test stage, the more useful the theories that survive will be. Rigorous statistics are valuable at this stage too.

6. Implement reinforces the whole purpose of the project in terms of bringing about robust and sustainable improvements to the organisation's processes. Whilst this may seem obvious, it is often the Achilles heel of many projects. Implementation must draw on the System of Profound Knowledge as the underlying principles for success, taking into account the wider system, the variation, operational definitions and of course the socio-emotional issues that will now be making their presence felt. The project team have the responsibility of understanding these principles in the context of the situation in which they find themselves. They then need to work by engaging local staff to introduce the changes successfully – using PDSA, of course. Only after a successful trial implementation should they consider wider, permanent changes to operating processes.

As with earlier stages you will recognise many parallels with your process management work. As also discussed before, the sequence of investigation, testing and implementation is much easier within a department than across functional boundaries. This is why it is so much better to come to a major improvement activity bolstered by such experience rather than learning about the whole subject from scratch in the high-pressure world of big projects.

Plans and reviews of the Implement stage must be developed closely with the sponsor and maybe other members of the senior management team. It is very likely that the actions will spread beyond the original scope, and this may irritate those who have not been kept on board. Even if they support the decisions, such widening scope may have implications for their resources, and if they are in the middle of some other change it may need the senior team to act as umpire.

7. Standardise recognises that when the team has translated an improvement theory into an improvement solution, they may have only resolved the issue for the short term. To ensure repeatability over the longer term, as discussed in Chapter 5, they must standardise the new process to reflect the improvements they have implemented. In some cases, this may involve a single process in a single site; in others it will involve transferring the learning across a number of sites in which parallel processes operate. Issues that are particular to each situation will arise. Contingency analysis tools can help prepare for the unexpected. The team needs to deal with these constructively so that the organisation can hold on to any new gains and ensure that it does not simply fall back into the old suboptimal ways of working. Often there needs to be a lot of effort to develop an integrated standardisation and maintenance process, supported by clearly defined roles and responsibilities.

Whatever the team or the top management hopes for, standardisation is rarely easy or quick, and it needs to be ready to take local circumstances into account – size or local laws may preclude uniformity. A 'roll-out' must not be thought of in terms of developing a solution and imposing it on every location; the later implementations must learn from the experience of the earlier ones, and indeed you may need to revisit the first few in the light of this learning.

8. Review enables the team to reflect upon the project in its wider sense. What have they learned about the organisation, and what have they learned about the improvement process? People will be able to see how the theories they held at the start of the project have developed as progress has been made. The summary report should highlight the key insights about how the organisation operates and what this might mean for subsequent improvement teams. They also need to review the process that the team went through to deliver the improvements achieved. Given that the improvement process sits within a wider support system, they must continually feed back learning about how to employ the improvement process within the organisation. This process itself will also need to evolve at least at the pace of the organisational system to remain relevant, but often it struggles to do so after the excitement of its early months. Finally, a review of what went well and what could be improved often highlights the people-centric issues that form the foundation of many of the problems that need to be overcome if the improvement programme is to yield its fullest potential.

It is important to celebrate the completion of a project. Team members need to feel appreciated, and others will feel more inclined to participate if they see that efforts are recognised. Such celebrations may take many forms, including conferences or articles in magazines as well as internal events. Someone should be given the task of writing the story of the project, the gains and the learning, to provide input to a growing database to which all can refer.

How Isaac Newton invented Lean Manufacturing, or the value of a learning approach regardless of the actual tools…

In a recent class I was asked to outline the history of Lean Sigma. Not many were expecting the story to start before the 1950s and some were looking at the mid-1980s. I was able to take them back to a story from more than three hundred years ago. Curiously, the purpose of this process is literally to make money.

It appears in a book by Thomas Levenson, called *Newton and the Counterfeiter* (Faber and Faber 2009). Born in 1642, Newton did his famous work in maths, physics and astronomy as a young man. He is regarded by many as one of the principal figures in developing the scientific method. He spent his middle age in trying to transmute elements – practising alchemy, in fact. But he was a genuinely scientific alchemist, testing theories and ultimately realising the challenge was impossible. So when, in his fifties, he was appointed Master of the Royal Mint with the task of rebuilding the credibility of the nation's currency he had the right background for the task, though no one could know it at the time.

Minting coins is a fairly straightforward system, starting with melting, followed by rolling, then punching and finally 'finishing'. It is not very different to this day. The requirement in May 1696 was to make £7million of coin, and the machines installed could only produce £15,000 per week but were not achieving even that. The plant was worn out, morale poor and corruption rampant. In theory it would thus require over nine years (in a country in which hardly any coins were available), and the treasury was demanding acceleration to £30,000 or £40,000 per week. The army was going unpaid and ordinary people had to barter to make trades.

Newton approached his task with 'the rigour instilled by decades of painstaking laboratory work ...' He got his hands dirty as a matter of principle. His rule was to 'trust no other's calculations, nor any other eyes but your own.' In our terms, this involves applying the PDSA cycle. Here we have 'go and see', but centuries ago. Newton applied the same empiricism he had learned in his laboratory to getting investment money from his bosses, bosses who were extremely reluctant to admit the need.

After his investigations he invested in the melting processes with new furnaces, and in rolling and stamping equipment. Most impressive perhaps, to those of us who have worked on accelerating production, was his study of the stamping process which he identified as the critical point of the whole system. He timed the operations and found the perfect pace, the drumbeat of just less than the heart rate that enabled the men to sustain their work hour after hour.

By the late summer of 1696 (in other words, only three or four months after the start) the production rate had apparently increased from £17,000 to £100,000 per week, enabling the recoinage to 'race ahead of its schedule'. As well as the satisfaction of the government, here is also a case where the original target was in fact much too modest, however impossible it seemed at the start. The lesson is that although the need was desperate, any target for output rates was bound to be meaningless – and this is usually the case in the twenty-first century.

These principles had to be rediscovered in the twentieth century in making automotive parts or dispatching planning documents. This challenge illustrates many aspects of a successful improvement project, in a political climate even more extreme than most twenty-first-century improvement managers could imagine. There was also the distraction of massive counterfeiting, and the French were constantly threatening to overwhelm the British and their allies.

Those who are developing their practice in business improvement should take considerable heart from this. We hear about apparently intractable problems, cultural barriers, investment restrictions and so on. Many do not even start in the face of such difficulties. Newton's story reassures us that the techniques of understanding the flow of the process, its waste and its data, and using these in designing simple experiments, are timeless. In his case the pressures were enormous; the political restrictions had led his predecessors to give up. But he got money where others had failed by using evidence. He built commitment from workers, which had not even been thought of before, by applying himself visibly on the production floor.

A final thought is that Newton's key asset, as well as his persistence, was to get to the nub of the problem by observation, relying on no one else's data, and building theories to explain it. He did not have the advantage of our improvement tools, but he was confident of his principles.

Attributes for successful improvement team leaders

Selecting the right kind of person as project leader is as important as it ever was: no amount of project management process, systemic thinking or technical skill takes away the importance of the demeanour of a particular person. In our experience really successful improvement team leaders exhibit a high proportion of the following attributes/skills. As you scan through the list below you will conclude that such people are rare, and are probably already in an important role from which it will be hard to get them released, and you will be right to do so. It's often been observed that those who are easily available are probably not right for the job. Ignoring this rule is of course one of the reasons why organisations that attempt multiple cross-functional projects usually fail to do justice to them.

Personality:

- Enthusiastic, self-motivated, driven to achieve important objectives.
- Takes personal accountability/responsibility for their actions and those of their team.
- Credible in the eyes of their peers and managers, confident in their own ability and that of others to succeed.
- Able to weather tough times and knockbacks and can also take personal feedback in a constructive manner.
- Challenges organisational assumptions and beliefs that are holding them back.
- Assertive but supportive and helpful to others.
- Enquiring, doesn't accept things on face value, not afraid to ask questions and listens actively.
- Seeks to understand different perspectives and points of view.
- Wants to understand why things are the way they are.
- Values learning and development for themselves and for others.

Operating style:

- Demonstrates leadership: communicates a compelling vision for improvement and is able to identify what needs to happen to achieve it.
- Able to follow a systematic approach to project work.
- Can organise themselves and others:
  - ◆ Can plan a work stream of activity, i.e. multiple tasks and milestones for multiple people.
  - ◆ Ability to delegate tasks and responsibilities.
- Can carry out basic data analysis.
- Good at communicating – both written and verbal.
- Able to present to small audiences of both peers and managers.
- Understands the organisational structure and work; knows who to ask.
- Able to lead a team of people and work as a team member.
- Seeks help as called for, both in technical subjects and personal coaching.

Relationships:

- Seeks to create alignment and consensus in thinking, able to build rapport with people at all levels of the organisation.

- Engages people from the peer-to-peer perspective, regardless of rank.
- Values others' knowledge and experience.
- Empathises with others' situations, feelings, thoughts, etc.
- Able to influence others without needing executive authority.

Nobody possesses all these characteristics, of course, but you will not regret using the list as a filter and incorporating the role in your career development process.

Reviewing project progress at gateway points

The Improvement Cycle itself provides gateways at the end of each phase that are natural points for reviews. These should include representatives from the top team and senior manager stakeholders. The following questions provide the basis of an agenda for such a review meeting;

- Reminder of objectives. (What are we trying to accomplish? How do we know if a change is improvement?)
- Achievements.
- Issues identified.
- Risks.
- Support required.
- Next steps proposed.
- And, of course, the learning the team has gained.

Make sure that the reviews are presented on wall displays and not in presentations, and generate discussion amongst the audience rather than passive acceptance.

The Improvement Cycle structure has been applied to a multitude of subjects. From improving response times in call centres to reducing energy consumption in paint spray booths, from rationalising product codes across a global chemical company to getting ships to arrive on time in port. To adapt a well-known catchphrase: 'Can it help you? Yes it can!'

Ann's reflections

Ann was now really sure that the principles of the System of Profound Knowledge, together with many of their tools, enabled a similar approach to be taken in both everyday work and major change projects. She had seen managers and staff using a common language, exploring opportunities and challenges with the same concepts, and applying their training with minimal adjustments.

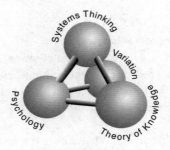

Looking back at the project she was elated, experiencing something of the epiphany that she had heard described by others. She now had quite a few people around her who did not want to go back to the old ways. Definitely ready for presenting to a conference!

Systems thinking:
- They had been able to manage projects in the context of the overall organisation and its strategy. It had not been easy; in fact, it had been quite a rollercoaster as people veered between 'getting on with it' and taking their time in order to engage others properly.
- She, and a few others, had begun to see an improvement project as a mini system with all that implied. She still wondered how to do better at balancing between maintaining a project's identity and it not becoming too detached from the ongoing work and people.

Variation:
- 'On target with minimum variation' had worked really well as a rallying call. In fact she was hearing it quoted at her by people who didn't know she had been the first to introduce it.

- The team had done well at pursuing sources of variation upstream, and developing new standard operations; now it was back to maintaining the standards.

Theory of knowledge:

- PDSA had featured at every stage, sometimes being repeated as needed, and they had tested to try and disprove the solutions. Some of the team were getting so vocal in their enthusiasm that she would have to get them to hold back a bit so as not to intimidate those who had not had much involvement.
- Operational definitions were another idea that had gripped the team, again perhaps too much right now, but hopefully they would find a balance.

Psychology:

- 'Sponsors, leaders, facilitators and team members need to be supported in both skills and personal interactions.' Yes, but that was hard to do; they had got away with some failings, but a lot more attention and skills would be needed if the activity was to grow.
- Great care had been taken to inform those affected in the project, both in trials and investigations and through to the implementation, and it had been worthwhile but very time consuming. Next time they would need to get more resources for this aspect.

9 Transforming over the longer term

It is good to have an end to journey toward; but it is the journey that matters, in the end.
Ernest Hemingway, writer, 1899–1961

Ann's story

'I'd like you to take on the job of divisional improvement director.' Ann gathered her thoughts quickly. This was not the time to hesitate, but she needed to think and didn't want to give the impression of dithering. Another year on and she was sitting in the CEO's office, all very comfortable, a cup of coffee and biscuits on the table in front of the sofas. Not many people got to meet him in his office, and those who did were normally sitting up straight in front of his big desk.

'I'd like you to take on the job of divisional improvement director.' The words echoed around her head. She had thought the meeting would be about some budget problems, and she had come ready with numbers and plans, justifications and reluctant proposals. It wasn't fair, she had thought, we had achieved so much but couldn't quite hit the targets – which she had never really agreed to in the first place. Her boss had not been much help. He said he didn't know what the meeting was for but was always happy to avoid confrontation, so she wasn't surprised he hadn't come along too. And here she was, being offered the best job of her career so far. But was it? The previous improvement director had left under something of a cloud, a pleasant enough man, but often pushed around and rather too theoretical in the face of challenge.

All these thoughts racing through her head in a flash; how long had she stayed silent, she had to get back in the room? 'Gosh, can you tell me some more?' she said. At least she hadn't said no, which was her first thought. It's a poisoned chalice, everyone knew that. She wildly thought of that sweepstake again; this job might generate a new one. But maybe if she kept the conversation going she might find out how to position it better. And even a couple of years in such a job would open up opportunities across the company, or in any company for that matter. Besides, you didn't turn down job offers in this company if you hoped to progress. You didn't get a second chance.

'Well, it's no good carrying on like we have been doing,' he said. 'We've got to change, and I need a right hand man, or woman, sorry, and we think you are the one.' 'We?' she said and went on, 'What sort of changes are you thinking of?'

Transforming a wider system

This is nearly at the end of the book, and we have arrived at the point at which many books start – the idea of completely refashioning an organisation. There's no shortage of examples on a grand scale, written up in books[5] and presented at conferences across the world. But, as we have said earlier, when you look closely at most of them the story doesn't usually hold together. There are plenty of accounts of programmes and their gains but not so much about enduring and continuing transformation. It is all too often the case that credit for the gains is claimed by many people, whilst blame for any shortcomings is aimed at the 'programme'. The change agents and consultants get a lot of criticism too, but probably not the executive leadership. As you have become more involved with radical change you probably have realised that all is not necessarily as it seems in the headlines and will have come to appreciate the value of having learned about it at a smaller scale.

You have undergone a practical apprenticeship with what you have done so far: making your work work better by understanding it, increasing readiness to change enough for modest changes to be accepted and generating stability. You've demonstrated methods for turning problems into opportunities for permanent improvement. You have taken this further by working at a larger scale beyond your own executive responsibility, and creating step changes in performance – and maintaining those too. This will most likely have stretched the tolerances of some of those both directly involved and on the fringes, who are not so ready for change and are happy to let others take the risks; they may even be jealous. You may be well aware that further effort may generate further resistance unless the whole organisation can be mobilised.

---

5 For instance *Built to Last*, Collins and Porras, 1994

We can consider the challenges of long-term strategic transformation through the use of the concepts and models introduced earlier.

Three levels of improvement

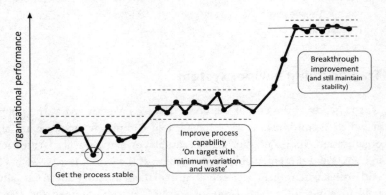

You have progressed from the left hand side of this graphic through to the right, and should feel confident that the methodologies and tools have even more potential. Many programmes simulate heroic ambitions and radical reorganisation – the right hand side – without any idea of what it needs to do just to get stable. It's hardly surprising that so many fail after a year or two. They tend to generate so many changes that the bottom part of the hamburger model – the socio-emotional issues – undermines the chance of success before the programme managers have even realised they have to take them into account. One breakthrough improvement is a reasonable expectation. Performing the trick multiple times over the whole organisation, and making it stick, requires a lot of effort and skill, and hence leadership. That leadership needs to be learned by the senior team; it will not happen spontaneously.

Increasing readiness to change

At this stage you, with your newfound and justified confidence, and perhaps a few others who have experienced and seen the benefits of sufficient change, will be hungry to apply it more widely. You all know how to make any work work better. It's time to consider how ready other influential people are for the kind of changes you have in mind.

The model for building readiness to change is even more important at this scale than when you considered it within your department.

The efforts you have been making to involve senior people, customers, suppliers and so on should pay dividends as your ambition grows. The top management team may at last be ready to consider taking a new approach if they are now sufficiently dissatisfied with the performance of the organisation and are aware of the achievements and potential of the process management approach. If you have kept good records of the situation before you started, and have accumulated evidence to show that the changes you led really are improvements, then you are on the way to addressing the future state vision – getting the organisation to be 'on target with minimum variation and waste'. That's just the start, however; now you need to consider building sufficient confidence in a comprehensive transformation to be able to get commitment to launch a programme that will take years to permanently change the way work is actually done. It calls for a robust methodology to provide structure and discipline in what will always be rather uncertain circumstances that therefore require continual learning on the way.

The Three-Question Model

The Three-Question Model can guide the development of a transformation strategy just as it does so well for a meeting or a problem.

- What are you trying to accomplish? Whilst every organisation must of course create its own vision, the Four Es (as discussed in Chapters 1 and 8) should be borne in mind.
- How will you know if the changes are improvements? The organisation is achieving its goals, and can demonstrate its management and improvement approach Everywhere, Everyday, by Everyone, for Ever. At this high level you will need both performance targets and some kind of value judgements, such as those in the process maturity table later in this chapter.

● What changes can you make that will result in improvements? The PMI Transformation Pathway described below provides structure for a multitude of changes to be tested rapidly, validated, modified and integrated as the learning and achievements progress.

True transformation must continually challenge assumptions

Any transformation is a journey that develops as the challenges are dealt with. At first it seems as though there are transactional changes that can be implemented, but it usually turns out that the barriers to doing so were hidden. Some of these may be rational, subject to evidence and testing by using PDSA. But many changes will step on someone's 'emotional toes', and may falter for lack of commitment when a problem is encountered. Such crises demand careful exploration on behalf of the sponsors of the programme and the facilitators. Some examples of these we recall include:

● Rationalising global product code descriptions – an apparently straightforward, if tedious, task but necessary to present a globally consistent multiproduct service on the web. However, one national operation had just been taken over and considered the demand to give up its product code format to be an intrusion on its independence. Much lack of cooperation led to interminable delays.
● A manufacturing company had been taken over and the new owners wanted to implement production line visual checks that included items which end users could not see. The new owners had already discovered that these check items were good indicators of overall quality, but the subsidiary managers were not prepared to allocate the resources to do this 'waste of time' work. Much aggravation resulted and the company did not survive – this was but one such intractable barrier.
● Support process managers such as finance, safety and HR who could not see themselves as providing enabling services to the manufacturing functions that actually produce the added value. Manufacturing managers resented the time taken to satisfy demands that had nothing to do with the customer and refused to cooperate when asked in the wrong way.

Such incidents do not always directly lead to corporate failure, but they do indicate critical leadership issues that had to be addressed, and meanwhile they undermined the transformation programme. Time spent

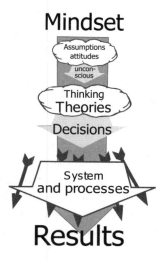

Mindset

Assumptions
attitudes

uncon-
scious

Thinking
Theories

Decisions

System
and processes

Results

on anticipating such issues, and on developing processes that ensure the leadership becomes quickly aware and deals with them, is time well spent. As the graphic above shows, it can often be the case that people do not realise what lies behind their discomfort – their assumptions are subconscious. And even if they become aware of their assumptions, they may not be aware that these determine all kinds of decisions that should be treated more openly.

Programme Pathway

This is a step-by-step journey that builds from comparatively modest beginnings to a comprehensive programme. It ensures that the organisation can learn about itself, deciding what kind of activities and behaviours it will need in the future, with time to develop them, both in the top team, other managers and the change agent resource, as the programme develops.

Act
Plan
Study
Do

In fact, even when an organisation makes a big commitment to a long-term programme it is important to keep a sense of proportion at first. Leaders may have decided on the need for a programme either in response to multiple critical problems or through an awareness that they need to manage for standardisation or stability. In either case, no matter how enthusiastic the sponsor of such a programme is, you can be certain that other senior people will be biding their time. They will probably have seen previous ambitious schemes fall away after a year or two. Most managers are skilled at keeping their heads down until the latest fad goes away and they can get back to the old ways again.

What is therefore needed is an approach that can be self-funding, and links the initial 'act of faith' declaration to learning by doing and paying by delivering. Acts of faith are essential at first but the programme will run into a crisis at some stage, so methodologies that produce tangible gains to go with improved culture have the best chance of thriving. In fact, it always takes a crisis to get people's attention to the implications of a change. In our experience, only then are they prepared to engage in dialogue about what things need to be like beyond next quarter's deadlines.

Transformation development

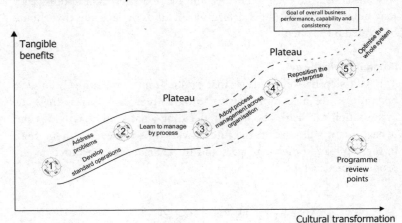

A transformation is thus always a journey of discovery and it can never end, as you will find when you talk with people involved with the best organisations – as you must; see Chapter 10. At every stage there are competing factors of degree of readiness to change, knowledge about progress and challenges, and understanding of the human factors to be addressed. These combine in making each journey unique, and even when the initial goals are reached it is always clear that more can be done, and that it will need modifications to the approach taken so far in order to do it.

For instance, in many transformations there is an initial programme of training and projects that produce good results and lots of enthusiasm if done well. But after six to nine months there will be turnover of staff and new challenges. The training of replacement staff must be addressed systematically, and those who move into new jobs require new training. This may mean that the transfer of training responsibility is passed from the transformation programme to the HR function, and they may not understand the implications. So unless you engage the HR managers with the spirit of the programme it will falter.

The Transformation Pathway addresses these issues by building awareness of the inevitability of plateaux as the programme moves on, no matter what the starting intentions were.

- For instance, after a campaign of initial projects and training people, you should become more conscious of the need to ensure that the future processes are stable and capable of maintaining the improved performance. In turn, it shows that people will find it difficult to keep individual processes stable without a supportive system, ranging from leadership behaviours to related enabling processes.
- On the other hand if the initial aim was to generate effective process management, this work will highlight urgent problems to be addressed before standardisation can effectively start.

Developing better enabling processes for particular parts of the business often generates benefits in other areas which have yet to receive attention. It becomes clear that all of the principal processes will need to be addressed, which means the whole organisation should be thought of in system terms. Eventually nothing short of transformation of the whole system can satisfy the ambition.

The phases of the Transformation Pathway provide a way of thinking about progress at this wide scale that is complementary to those described earlier in relation to local process work. There are likely to be many plateaux in different places and at different times. Each is a warning that progress has stalled, and something new needs to happen to break out of the impasse. If the warning is not heeded and a revised approach is not developed things will go backwards. It is at these critical stages, as well as in launching, that external consultants can be particularly valuable because they will have seen such symptoms before, as we discuss in Chapter 10.

Energy from the top is always critical. It is like the stages of an interplanetary space mission. If an organisation-wide programme is intended, it must receive sufficient initial investment commitment for it to reach the stability of an orbit. Then, when the next stage is to be fired it must again be of sufficient energy and duration that people believe it will continue towards the destination. And en route it must be adjusted to keep it on track toward its goal, and with enduring commitment at the top to learn – even when it is cruising. Later on in a programme it is not the lack of payback that brings the whole thing back to earth; it is not recognising it, and the consequent lack of appreciation from those at the top.

1. Launch the programme

Option 1. Address problems. An improvement programme is often stimulated by failures in performance, and thus would start with projects to address critical problems (just a few, see Chapter 8), with strong support and training provided to those involved – to make sure they succeed. If this is done well, there is a surge of activities and interest with positive outcomes.

Option 2. Standardise operations. An alternative trigger for a programme is the realisation that, even though an organisation is performing acceptably, it is inconsistent. In this case the leadership decides to embark on a programme of standard operations by developing a process management approach together with its required tools. This is also generally well received by those involved, but is almost certain to expose opportunities for improvement that go beyond standardisation and have implications across functions.

Readers will appreciate that either of these cross-functional programme contexts are different to the approach in this book. We have been addressing an individual manager operating without a supportive infrastructure, someone who can work within their area of responsibility to apply different methods. They can take time as appropriate to the scale of their particular challenge, and have no need to prove anything to anyone except their boss and their own people. A company-wide programme will have a much higher profile, and needs to demonstrate its value by addressing cross-functional problems that many people feel are intractable.

Whichever the starting point, a review – Study – is called for after a few months, and should be put in the diary at the start.

2. The first plateau

After the launch, with its associated training and application work, and probably some problems dealt with, there is often a pause whilst everyone catches their breath and wonders what comes next. A programme review typically reveals a series of judgements and realisations:

- If it was a problem-oriented start, there will be project benefits that are real and acknowledged, and the Improvement project methodology will be well appreciated by active participants. Senior managers may well be keen to expand project activities to deal with all kinds of problems, but will not know how to select the right ones. (These ambitions may still need holding back, depending on how many top managers are ready to learn to be good sponsors.)
- If it was a process-oriented start the methods and culture are also usually well received by those involved. However, there are probably not many tangible gains to offset against the investment, and there may be frustration building up if those problems that surfaced are not receiving sufficient attention.
- There is more readiness to consider the needs and wants of the customer, both internal and external.
- Leaders are learning the value of the universal common language, especially in large and multinational organisations.
- There is an appetite for more training / education in the process management and improvement approach.
- There is an acknowledgement of the value of a structured programme for the work and for good leadership of it.

However, at this stage, and no matter how positive the feedback, the approach is only partially internalised; it has not become the default way of working, especially when under pressure.

People are starting to realise that stable, standardised processes are necessary to retain the gains they have made and reduce the need for major problem-solving projects in future.

In summary, no matter what the achievements, practice is still varied and achievements are fragile. The leaders' experience has led them to see that 'there is another way', but they are probably not seeing it clearly and are not sure what to do next.

The consequence of these characteristics is that, although the organisation has made progress – with some genuine achievements and a new confidence – it has reached a plateau. It has found out how to solve big problems but not how to prevent them developing in the first place. Changes of policy as well as activities are needed if the gains are to be retained and built upon.

Depending upon the readiness to change of the whole organisation, the programme leaders may decide to revisit their starting point, filling in the gaps exposed no matter what was the first emphasis. This builds more evidence to support the next push forward.

3. Secure the gains, adopt process management across the organisation

The whole organisation evidently needs a comprehensive and rigorous approach to managing processes to build upon the achievements so far and be ready for more. It needs to learn about the nitty-gritty of everyday cross-functional process management that complements the methods and tools proven in the project work. This is not to say that the work already started should not carry on as before – far from it. There will still be more opportunities for breakthrough improvement than the organisation can handle, and if they are properly selected, supported and learned from, the properly completed ones reinforce the whole message.

The process-management phase of the programme consists of policy decisions about process ownership, extensive training in process management alongside continuing training for those involved with projects, and increasing coaching of leaders to incorporate the new approach in their everyday jobs. It is likely to ask awkward questions about functional responsibilities, management hierarchies and so on.

Many of the achievements of this phase will take the form of deepening those already in progress. These are **emphasised**:

- Project benefits are recognised as real and acknowledged, the method is appreciated, and projects have been repeated and **some are written up.**
- There is more emphasis on the customer, and **customers are noticing the difference.**

- Leaders realise that stable, standardised processes are necessary to retain the gains, and have **personally led such processes through crisis** and difficulty.
- Training and education includes much more content for **everyday process management**. All training in other disciplines incorporates aspects of process understanding and improvement. For example, this includes subjects such as health and safety, sales, design, projects, recruitment and finance.
- **Managers have substantially justified to themselves**, and can explain to others, the claim that stable / standardised processes reduce the need for major problem-solving projects.
- There is **acknowledgement of the value** of a programme for the work and for good leadership of it. However, there may still be frustration at the pace and much need for support for individuals.
- The approach is internalised and is becoming the default approach, **especially when under pressure.**
- Much **management practice is standardised,** achievements are robust; effectiveness is seen as the route to efficiency, and capability is being translated into ability.

In summary, by this time the leaders can describe their personal role in the change, and they know there is even more potential. They are confident about what to do next.

4 and 5. Reposition the enterprise, optimise the whole system

The experience of earlier phases of the pathway will lead to an increased realisation of the limitations of the organisation's structures and strategies. Leaders and practitioners will find that continuing progress is increasingly being impeded by contradictions across the organisation. Contradictions can include managing by departmental budget, manipulation of data and pressure on projects to deliver before they have run their trials. Any one of the traditional top-down management behaviours can get in the way. If top management does not address the contradictions, frustration builds and achievements plateau once again; they may even go downhill.

It is at this stage that the foundations which you have established will bear fruit for the organisation. The common language helps people see that the principles are valid and that the methods will help address the deepest of strategic problems. Top management teams that call upon the expertise find that they can make unprecedented changes with the help of their people and are not in conflict with them as has often been the case in the past.

This concept of programme development enables you to be aware of the stage of your own thinking and to anticipate the greater scope and ambition that each review will reveal. It has much in common with the AGILE approach to software development.

Assessing progress

Part of the dialogue with those who are reluctant to change involves the clarification of evidence of the benefits which the traditionalists will probably downplay. Throughout all this work there is a critical need to keep track of achievements and learning. Everyone, from the most junior clerk to the most senior director, needs encouragement to keep on with changing by appreciating what is being gained, both tangibly and intangibly.

There are plenty of corporate assessment processes such as the Business Excellence Model in Europe, the Malcolm Baldrige National Quality Award in the US and the Deming Prize (now the Deming Grand Prize) across Asia, and references are given in the appendix. They have all been useful, but have also been used in some cases for the glory of the prize rather than the real transformation of the performance of the organisation on behalf of the customer. In addition, the ISO 9XXX series of standards or ISO 140001 Environmental standards provide a more transactional and less heroic framework for testing progress.

Organisations may decide to work towards winning one or other of these prizes or certificates as a way of gaining recognition and reputation. However, all of them are costly and slow. In addition, as anyone who has studied the examination culture knows, such awards may indicate more about a talent for winning awards or being in compliance with requirements than of transformation. Thinking back to the Four-Student Model, lots of kids with good grades struggle in real life, and countless kids with poor exam results thrive later on.

We think it most useful for an organisation to understand its own achievements first, and then apply for an award when it is confident it is doing so for the right reason. You can use some of the approaches already described to judge progress and needs for change to make better progress.

How are you doing in relation to the Four Es?

'The organisation is achieving its goals, and can demonstrate its management and improvement approach Everywhere, Everyday, by Everyone, for Ever.'

Two components of transformation are tracked in this way, results and method. If the organisation is achieving its goals, that's great – but it may just be luck; it may suffer when times get hard. But if the organisation does understand the contribution of the approach we have been describing you can be very confident in predicting that the improvements will pay dividends though bad times as well as good.

Performance characteristic visible	Contribution of major projects	Contribution of process management
Everywhere. Across the whole organisation, including strategy development, everyday work and projects.	Projects are multifunction, with strategic goals, solutions are implemented into everyday processes.	All can see how they contribute to the optimisation of the organisation, either in delivering added value to the customer / end user, or in enabling the delivery processes.
Everyday. Leaders understand and can explain the relationship between how they approach their work and the overall improved results they have achieved.	In order for the changes to be permanent leaders have had to make links between methods behind the achievements of the projects and their implementation into daily management.	Daily process management delivers products and services predictably, responds to problems as they arise before they impact on customers.
By **Everyone.** The approach is used in depth where appropriate, and can be explained by line managers and staff routinely, not just the improvement personnel.	Active sponsorship by top management ensures they understand that the approach is different. Continual review of the improvement process means that all involved have helped adapt the approach and don't have to rely on specialists.	People are trained in methods to analyse their processes and their data, and have the will and the permission to improve locally, and to contribute cross-functionally.

For **Ever.** It has clearly been applied and developed over many years.	As the larger-scale projects take root, and the approach is used again and again, participation becomes part of everyone's career development.	'This is how we do things here.' Newcomers are properly inducted; non-adopters have gone.

We find that these four fields of judgement make sense to ordinary managers, of whatever seniority.

Review process maturity

In Chapter 1 we introduced the idea of a graduated series of levels of maturity, and hopefully you made some notes then. Now is the time to refer back, comparing how things seem to be now with how they looked then. You may find, as many others have, that you now think you were too generous at first. As you learn more about process management you also learn that the potential is more than you could ever have conceived. This goes with being a very hard taskmaster when you visit other work sites – or shops, airports, banks, sports clubs… You also have to learn to keep a sense of proportion and humour, or get a reputation for obsessiveness!

Four-Student Model

We introduced this concept in Chapter 1. It takes us beyond the raw impressions created by achievement or failure, by asking both 'how did we do?' and 'did we go about it as we intended?'. This pair of questions lie at the heart of all good coaching by getting the individual to think through the 'hows' as well as the 'how muches'. A tennis player will try and recall if they threw the ball up in just the right way for the serve when the ball misses the service line. A golf player might try and recall whether they kept their head down when a shot flies over the green. A meeting manager should think about the steps they took in preparation before the meeting that ended in confusion – had they the right attendees, was the agenda clear, did they check on what they were trying to accomplish at the start of the meeting, not half way through or after that confusion?

The Four-Student Model provides a reminder that we can learn when things don't go as expected, but that we learn little if they run smoothly unless we take the steps to articulate what was different to our previous behaviour.

Level	Meaning	Comments at time of first study	Comments after establishing process management	Comments after transformation work
1	The key processes are identified.			
2	Ownership of them has been established, and their purpose is understood.			
3	They are formally flowcharted / documented and standardised operations can be seen.			
4	Appropriate and visible measures are used to monitor the processes and enable learning.			
5	Feedback from customers, suppliers and other processes is sought and used as the basis for improvement.			
6	An improvement and review mechanism is in place with targets for improvement.			
7	Processes are systematically managed for continual improvement, and learning is shared.			
8	The processes are benchmarked against best practice.			
9	The processes are regularly challenged and re-engineered if required.			
10	The processes are a role model for other organisations.			

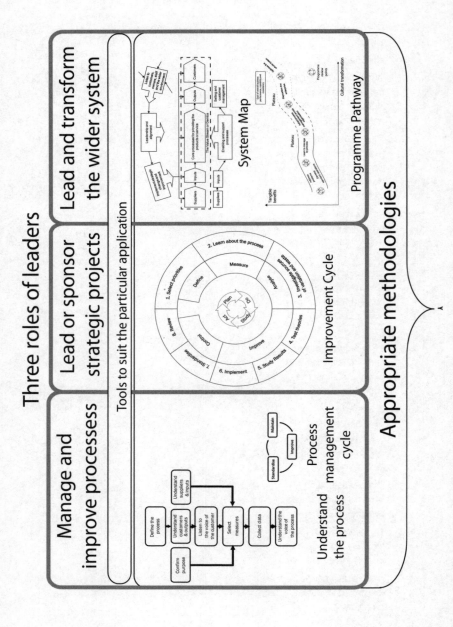

Three roles of leaders

Manage and improve processess

Lead or sponsor strategic projects

Lead and transform the wider system

Tools to suit the particular application

Understand the process

Process management cycle

Improvement Cycle

System Map

Programme Pathway

Appropriate methodologies

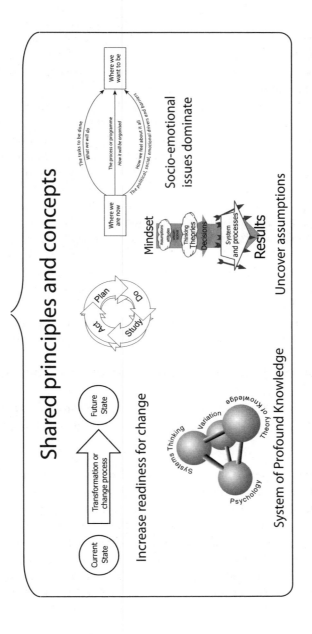

143

Transformation demands all three types of leader

We have seen how the basic requirement of a line manager is to ensure that their work produces the outputs required by the customer, alongside the associated demands of managing people, reporting results and so on. Many people spend much of their career fulfilling this role, responding to problems and hopefully cooperating with major changes as they are introduced.

We have also seen how such a manager has the opportunity to lead in escalating problems or opportunities beyond their immediate responsibilities, and participate in or lead longer-term, cross-functional projects that lead to process redesign. If they have explored and applied the process management approach in their everyday work they find it powerful in the project environment.

Developing a longer-term strategy uses exactly the same principles, but with additional methodologies to guide the use of the tools.

This graphic of the roles of managers and leaders expands on the summary version used earlier. It is a key piece of evidence for our assertion that the System of Profound Knowledge, with constant use of PDSA, can be a universal foundation for all your work. Those who have conquered the challenges of getting processes 'on target with minimum variation and waste', and keeping them there, have completed an apprenticeship that puts them in a strong position when a top management opportunity comes along.

Developing your career by leading and facilitating

This section is relevant in larger organisations, demonstrating routes to senior jobs based upon a series of increasing responsibilities and variety of challenges.

Top line management jobs must not be junior jobs at a larger scale

Those running everyday processes are inevitably preoccupied with their immediate results. They spend their time with their people, chasing routine performances, troubleshooting the local technologies and placating customers. This is entirely understandable: they are accountable for particular outputs, and whilst we encourage them to look beyond their immediate horizons, they must not lose sight of the task in hand. A local manager's involvement with change may well be as a participant rather than a leader.

A manager promoted to supervise a set of local managers can often thrive with much the same approach, albeit with a wider range of contacts across the organisation. They may or may not be proactive in leading improvement, depending upon their disposition and experience.

The job of a top manager should be very different. They must take a broad view of the organisation; indeed, if they are a director they have an obligation to work to optimise the whole system, rather than merely championing their own part. They must consider the future of the organisation and even the future of the societies in which they operate, such as changing markets, technologies and social trends. They must try to define the future state of the organisation, and to lead it, or parts of it, through the transformational changes they consider to be needed.

Thus a board meeting is, or should be, much more than just a meeting of department heads. Reviewing current performance should be a minor part of the process. The bulk of the time needs to be spent considering the longer term, addressing learning from current operations, the strategy, and the change programmes that are intended to deliver the transformation. Time and energy taken in arguing about and manipulating immediate results and prospects leaves that much less for efforts to develop a capable system for the future. We have all too often seen top teams exhausted by the pressure of today's numbers, with no appetite for the puzzles of changing their organisation and themselves. Part of their transformation needs to be on changing that emphasis, no matter how hard it seems to be; they will have no future if they don't spend constructive time working on it.

In our experience this shift in the emphasis of meetings from local to board level is poorly understood, and rarely practised. Many top managers understandably stick with the behaviours that got them promoted. Top management meetings are all too often very similar to department meetings, with bigger numbers, louder voices and the stronger egos that top managers often seem to think are needed. There is an atmosphere of immediacy: times are always hard, money is always tight. 'Don't you understand, we have to deliver this year's results, we don't have the time to reflect on the year after next?'

A cross-disciplinary approach to career development

You will be able to be very different – because of your experiences in using PDSA, and associated methodologies and tools to progress from problem solving through maintaining process performance to participating or

145

leading major cross-functional projects. You will have demonstrated to yourself, and to others, that the same approach to leading everyday management also works in leading continuing radical change.

The model below shows how you and the organisation can take advantage of this universality – developing a standard approach to both everyday and change management – to help individuals in their career development from the moment of their joining the organisation, no matter how junior they may be.

Career development cycling from line to change manager

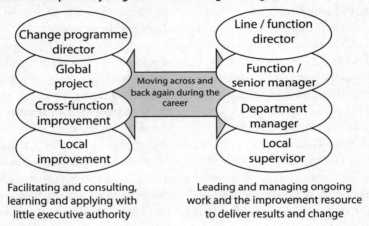

A person can start their career either in a support function, helping local supervisors to learn about and improve their processes, or in the supervisory function itself. After some time in either of these roles they can transfer to the other one and their experience will enrich this next step. And so on through the organisation. At every level, regardless of being either a line manager with change experience or a change manager with line experience, the mixture of skills and behaviours makes for a more effective person in their current role. Just as importantly, their experience in each role makes them much better at relating to the other people they encounter: the politics and emotions of the relations between change agents and line managers are famously tricky. Those who have done both become better clients to the change agents, and better change agents to the clients.

The culmination of this career development is that the CEO has experience of keeping the show on the road, using principles, logic and tools, and of leading people in building new roads, using the same principles, logic and tools. They use consistent language and appreciate the different challenges of their generalists and specialists. They have a head start in any relationship with consultants and trainers, for they have switched between being poacher and gamekeeper for many years and have learned how to make the best of any available help.

Ann looks back

Two years on, and Ann was putting her things into boxes, getting ready to move to the new job the next week. A further step up, and a seat on the managing board – maybe a new sweepstake, she thought, as she put the envelope into the box of mementos to take home. Maybe not; there was no doubt they had achieved a lot in the couple of years, though she had a nagging sense that she was leaving a bit too soon for the effort to be self-powered from here. But she didn't want to get labelled as a change specialist just yet; she felt she could make more of a contribution as a senior line manager now she had so much background in charge.

One of the drawers had the notes for the conference speech she had given a couple of months ago; she had wondered at the time whether this might stimulate a new job offer. She had of course done the summary around the System of Profound Knowledge, trying to capture the key learning amongst all the activities, achievements and setbacks.

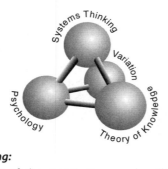

Systems thinking:

● 'The purpose of the organisation needs rethinking.' She felt they had a much better sense of what they could achieve if they really committed to optimising, but the existing goal still talked in clichés about 'shareholder value' and 'sustainability' without being sufficiently specific so that people would know they had to change.

- 'The structure of the organisation will also need redeveloping.' This was for sure; the historic functional divisions are divisive, resources are not balanced, relationships are strained as directors fight their corners, defend their spheres of power and influence. As from next week she would be in the thick of this fight, and her old boss was one of the worst offenders – of course.

Variation:
- 'We are intending to building a process-based organisation to achieve "on target with minimum variation and waste".' Hmm, fine words in her presentation, she thought, but not entirely supported by others who still found specifications more comfortable.
- 'We are aiming to make all our key processes "capable", i.e. they are stable and can satisfy their customers' requirements.' That was true; it was a plank in their strategy, but lots more training and relentless attention to detail was still needed. She looked forward to being the pathfinder.
- 'We are developing a culture of working to process.' Also true; an explicit goal in the strategy, but a lot of her senior colleagues still seemed to dive in without thought whenever something didn't fit with the budget or generated a complaint. Again, she would have to set the example, and realised it might not be so easy now she would be directly in the line of fire.
- 'We are working to eliminate arbitrary goals for departments and people.' Yes, that went down well at the conference; lots of questions about exactly what she was doing, and she was not so pleased with herself afterwards because it felt a bit smug. It was actually proving really hard to keep to sensible, customer- and staff-focussed goals which they were all sure would help in the long term. They didn't fit in the so-called Balanced Scorecard that had been (unhelpfully) in force for many years, and it looked like the new 'Operational Excellence' goals that were on the horizon would be different but no better. All these goals were deployed to divisional and departmental level, and led to narrow thinking and blame.

Theory of knowledge:
- 'Learning is at the heart of all planning and review activities.' Well, yes; this was much better than a couple of years ago. People enjoyed the

meeting processes, recognised how useful it could be to open up discussions on competing theories and carry out proper tests. But again, because these took time and money, there always seemed to be someone claiming that they could be accelerated or even done away with altogether. Another field in which she would have the chance to be a torchbearer...

Psychology:

- 'We sponsor routine two-way communication between levels and across functions.' Yes, they did. It hadn't been bad before, and was better now; all it needed was to be kept as routine over the months and years. No problem (!).

- 'Personal rewards are much more about gain-sharing based upon the organisation's performance, and less about individual targets.' She had taken a bit of licence with this claim. HR was actually pretty keen on this change and they were carrying out some trials, but the old bonus system was so entrenched that even those who knew it was faulty were unhappy with giving it up without guarantees. Much more to do here.

- 'Career progress is starting to reward those who learn and apply their talents to optimising the whole system.' Well, it was starting, and Ann was one of those benefitting. If they kept it up for ten years people would start to believe it.

10 Organising help

Discovery consists of seeing what everyone has seen, and
thinking what no one has thought.
Albert von Szent-Györgyi, biochemist, 1893–1988

The more you can see your work through the eyes of others the better
the chance you have of thinking what no one in your organisation has
thought before.

Ann's story

Soon after she had started the improvement director role, Ann
contemplated the pile of leaflets and printouts that she had accumulated,
each describing a particular company's approach to supporting change
and improvement programmes. Some were luxury brochures boasting
of 'global reach' and 'Sixty per cent of the Fortune 500' as clients. Others
simply listed the services they offered, but claimed to be the best
value – did they mean 'cheapest,' she wondered? Then there were the
companies that featured a jargon-filled offering: 'Six Sigma', 'Lean', 'Process
Engineering', 'Lean Sigma' – whatever such titles might mean. She had
heard of most already, but now she looked at the literature the same
words seemed to have varied meanings. Did they teach operational
definitions, she wondered. She looked again at the companies she had
already encountered. One or two she wouldn't readily work with again,
another couple had proven trustworthy but might be too 'different' for
her new boss. One thing was for sure, she would be insisting that any
provider could explain the underlying principles behind its work; she was
not impressed by rows of examples, or of fresh-faced graduates talking
up their change-management qualifications. Whoever it was would have
to be able to get alongside her senior colleagues and work with them on
her behalf; she knew that, as an insider, she could only get so far in their
personal change work.

She was three weeks into the job, and was still *Studying*, remembering
the value of getting an early impression of what was going on before taking
too many decisions. It wasn't the same as when she joined the organisation,
for she had already encountered many of the key people in the company,

but she was reassured by how different the conversations with them now were. Most said they welcomed her appointment, though one or two were pretty guarded and she wondered what problems they would cause. What was clear from her earlier experience was the need for training in improvement and change skills, and that the existing providers had not made a big impression. It was not so clear whether that was because of their lack of competence or commitment or her predecessor's inability to get the line managers fully supporting the programme and the right people in the post.

She wanted to enthuse managers to get on with working with PDSA, regardless of their knowledge of the techniques. She also wanted to expose people to a much wider range of other ideas, get them thinking at least a little differently.

Choosing a provider for an ongoing programme is a big decision for anyone. The future direction of the organisation depends on the abilities of the leaders to lead in a new way, and for all to use structured methodologies and tools at the right time and in the right manner. But the appointment should not be taken in isolation for there are many sources of free or very cheap knowledge, ideas and stimulus that should be worked with as well. All of them increase the chance of new eyes seeing old things and old eyes seeing new things. All they need is time.

Referring back to the start of this book, we made three assertions about transformation:

1. We can say with absolute certainty that you can rely on the principles if you use them properly, no matter what your work environment, culture or geography.
2. The methodologies that structure the application, from strategy to daily work, are tremendously robust when used properly.
3. The dozens of tools provide insight and discipline whenever they are used properly.

Once again, 'properly' is important! What follows helps you recognise and experience it, to practise it and lead others to join you.

Getting better at improving requires lots of practice

It's impossible to improve without changing, and it's impossible to be the best without being different.

These two truisms apply to the whole organisation, of course. They are what lie behind all so-called change programmes. But they apply equally to those who would lead change and improvement in organisations – they need to change their skills and behaviours. All your decisions therefore need to be focussed upon increasing readiness to change and getting commitment to the plans.

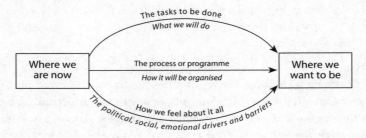

If you have been trying the methods through the book to this stage, you have been learning the skills of leading change both of yourself and your work environment. As with sport, artistic and craft skills, there is no substitute for this practice and much has been written about how much time is needed to become routinely competent. The 10,000 hours to become a top performer is a number often mentioned[6]. Whilst the exact number of hours is subject to much debate, it's a lot. If you spent half your work time practising (say twenty hours per week) it would take nearly seven years to get to just half the 10,000 hours. Those who spend ten per cent of their time in practising their skills are clearly still relative beginners after a year or two. It might not feel like it, for they may be better than when they started and the organisation might expect them to have become experts by then, but they have limited experience and limited ways of dealing with surprises.

However, practice time on its own is not the answer. I learned to play the guitar a little in my teens and have played quite a lot on and off since then, possibly 5,000 hours in fifty years. But I'm not very good! I became stuck at

---

6 *Outliers: The Story of Success*, Malcolm Gladwell; Little, Brown and Co, 2008

a basic level, so I took some lessons and progressed marginally, but I did not have enough time to practice and hence never internalised the new techniques. Over the years I have played for many hours – pretty much the same songs, of course – and enjoyed the sensation but have not got any better. I would starve if I tried to make a living. With nobody observing, advising and disciplining me, my ambition to play in a blues band is going to be unfulfilled. In fact, it's worse than that: I have practised so much in the wrong kind of techniques that I would need to unlearn a lot before I could get any better.

Sounds familiar? Most readers will have learned something in the wrong way, with bad habits, from swimming to tennis, to handwriting or singing, perhaps driving their car. They get along OK, but with no improvement over the decades.

Managers pick up a lot of experience over the years, but if it's not coached that will not help their practice very much.

So even a lot of unguided practice is not enough for being really good at the skills of leading and managing change. It's not easy, this change and improvement business, as you know from what you have been doing. The System of Profound Knowledge simplifies the task of building a curriculum by providing four categories, but there are a lot of skills to master. Few are difficult in themselves – just like kicking a football is not that difficult – but using them in the messy world of human interactions can be really hard when the pressure mounts. At times your work as a leader of change is going to require help in the form of skills by an expert who routinely uses them under pressure. Just like a surgeon working on an operation, you need somebody who last did the challenging task you have in mind for them yesterday afternoon and not three months ago. At other times you will be able to do a good job yourself if you take on a coach to help you prepare and review.

So you need to build competence within the organisation and should acknowledge that it will be years before you can rely on your own competences for everything, indeed if you ever can. Examples of where you need in-depth skills honed by years of experience include top management team facilitation and complex technical problem-solving statistics. They may always need to be provided by paid-for outsiders.

If all this seems like self-promotion from a consultant, so be it. But people do find that leading and facilitating change is really tough, so it would be wrong to give the impression they can learn it quickly and keep the programme on track when troubles occur, as they will.

Discovering and validating sources of help

We hope you are not surprised and maybe relieved to know that PDSA is the approach to take in this journey:

 Observe, read and listen, discover a useful person / idea / technique, etc.

 Make sense of the relevance and decide where it might be useful.

 Plan a trial of the help – 'What am I trying to accomplish, how will I know if the change is an improvement?'

 Carry out the trial / experiment and observe, collecting feedback.

 Reflect on the experience, and repeat – to validate it, or to apply it on a larger scale.

Developing skills in leadership, management, improvement and change programmes thus demands the use of PDSA with lots of practice, lots of feedback and taking risks but keeping them at a manageable level whenever possible. Use the Four-Student Model to take note of what worked and what didn't and why – was it the process or was it the execution? Every stage will be improved with help, and you can discover and validate the nature and source of that help with PDSA.

Here as elsewhere on this journey, persistence has a high value. The first test rarely works properly. People often don't return calls but that may not mean they are not interested; your item may fall off the agenda of someone else's meeting, and so on. Keep trying, don't take no for an answer, and don't take setbacks personally. A coach, formal or informal, can be a great help when times get frustrating.

Different forms of help

You need to move well away from your regular processes and contacts for some kinds of help and stay much closer to them for others.

Increasing dissatisfaction by observation and diagnosis of your processes and interactions. This needs someone detached who won't take things for granted and whose job is not dependent upon the good opinions of those being observed or questioned. This was the role you were taking in Chapter 1 at the start of your new job, but by Chapter 7 you were probably becoming too close to your own department. You now need outsiders to cast fresh light on what you are missing.

Discovering more attractive futures by encountering different ideas. You need to observe different organisations and activities if you wish to see or experience alternative ways of working or solving problems. What looks like innovation in one place often has its origins in practice elsewhere: existing ideas were refashioned in translation. This is not to advocate copying and pasting, of course – every circumstance is different. You learn to look at what others have seen and think differently about it because of your separation from it. There lies the basis of many an innovation.

Beware of thinking that you need to find a 'world class' organisation in order to learn something new, impressive or surprising. Good ideas can come from modest places. Equally, just because your organisation is market leading, don't think there's nothing to learn from competitors. Really successful people and organisations are always prepared to look beyond the glitter.

This whole concept has been called Benchmarking, and is sometimes marketed as a programme in itself. However, you can do a perfectly adequate job yourself initially, based upon process and variability questions. If you need to broaden the scope or accelerate the pace you then have a good basis for employing external support to help if you have done some yourself.

Developing new and better skills and behaviours. Having decided upon the need to be different, making the changes to one's personal behaviour requires support and stimulation from someone closely connected over an extended period of time. This may be a boss, a colleague or a paid-for coach or mentor. They need to be close enough and skilled enough to help you see yourself, and to guide you in discovering how to be different. Training is only the start; it is nothing like enough in itself.

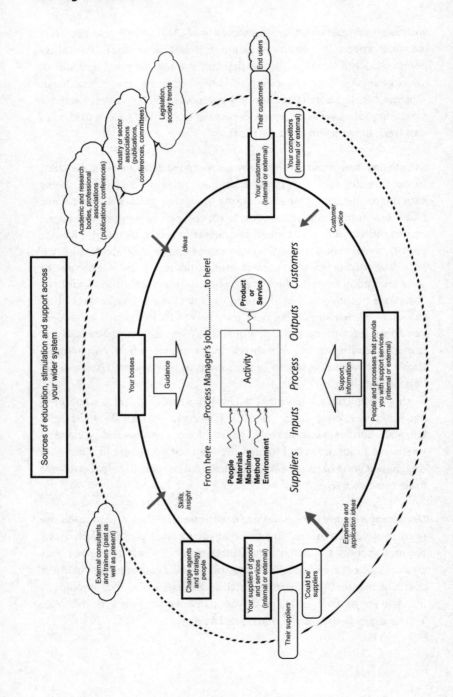

Sources of knowledge, ideas, examples...

We are all surrounded by people, processes and organisations that may be interesting and useful for both increasing dissatisfaction and envisaging a better future.

It's important to keep system thinking, process and variability questions in mind as you interact with outsiders. For instance you may see a presentation about a disaster on an oil rig, and be drawn to look for the parallels in the operations between the case study and your own organisation. If you do, you and your colleagues are likely to see reasons why you have little to learn because of the apparent differences: 'What have we got to learn from an oil company?'. You have to ask yourselves such questions as 'what varied?' or 'was this incident a surprise or just an unfortunate extreme of normal operations?' or 'were staff able to report concerns about near misses without feeling threatened?'. Then you will get answers that require further discussion and are likely to be universal in application.

You will recognise many of these categories and people from Chapters 1 and 2:

Customers, both internal and external. That's not just talking with them, but experiencing as far as possible. Make contact also with possible customers (who have reasons for not using your products or services) and ex-customers (whose reasons for leaving are almost certainly not the ones given by people in your organisation).

Suppliers, internal and external. Visit, listen, experience. In the same way as with customers, find suppliers who might deal with you but don't, and ask them why. Treat suppliers as experts – they should know more than you can ever know about what they do for you. If they are experts, what do they suggest they could do better for you, or that you could do better with their outputs? Any supplier who doesn't seem like an expert shouldn't be a supplier; their only qualification would then be cost, and that's no use in the long term. Listen to trainers and consultants, including managers of outsourced services, in the system; maybe take them out for a meal, you can learn a great deal in an informal setting.

Support or enabling services, who also may be internal or external. If they regard you as a customer you can bring the Kano model (see chapter 2) into the discussions. Engage in dialogue with them to uncover how you can optimise your interactions.

Trade associations and professional bodies are great sources of ideas, expertise and possibly mutual support. Reading magazines is a good way of accumulating knowledge at a sensible rate – over the years you can build up an impressive awareness of background. Conferences are good ways of listening to current issues but also of networking with like-minded people. Giving talks to conferences improves these networks and the preparation of a speech is one of the best ways of developing your own thinking, though make sure you test it with a colleague before delivering, see page 86. Take opportunities to meet and network with competitors too. Volunteering for regional, conference or national committees also builds networks, probably including a few people with whom you can exchange personal ideas. Best of all is to spend time as the chair of a committee, using it to experiment in a safe environment to develop your leadership approaches. This route also broadens your network to future employment; it certainly did for me.

Formal assessments, perhaps for ISO standards or quality awards, can provide dispassionate judgement of performance and suggestions for future improvement work. Assessors will have many ideas for improvements if you ask, even if it's not officially part of their remit.

Internal sources of advice, professional skills or training
These are there to help you and your colleagues make progress on the transformation journey.

Human Resources should be the first port of call for training and support. They may not have everything you need, but they should know where to look. It's likely that your exploration and needs will take you beyond the existing HR offerings list, but starting with cooperation puts you in the best position to ask for them to be open to new providers that you know of or discover.

Internal change agents. There is a huge range of scale and competence in change agent resources. Many large organisations will have improvement facilitators of one kind or another, but their qualifications require enquiry and demonstration before you can rely upon them. This graphic shows how they may be deployed.

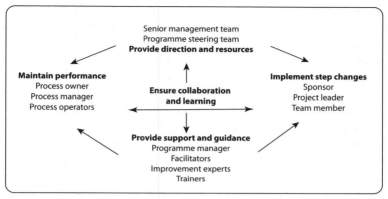

Leadership and change support roles in transformation

If you started your new job as a process-oriented manager, as outlined in the early chapters, you should find that change agents will welcome your request for help with open arms as you are someone who can speak their language. You will then be able to assess whether they are up to the task. We outlined the required attributes of a good project leader in Chapter 6, and any change agent should have many of those. A facilitator / change agent does not need the drive towards completion of a project leader, of course, but they do need a sense of humour and a desire to see you, the line manager, as their client.

When you select change agents be sure to keep the standards high, using the position to develop high flyers. Never fill a vacancy with someone who just happens to be available. If you are needing to recruit to make resources available, recruit into the line roles, releasing a good internal person as change agent. If you recruit outsiders into the change posts they tend to serve for a while and move elsewhere, and that's no way to build the culture for the long term. If, in the event, you do have to recruit outsiders as change agents make sure they are inducted into your programme's principles. They must not think that they can simply import whatever approach they had before.

Other support functions and processes. You will have met some of these in learning about your processes. In our experience, managers throughout the organisation will be pleased to help if asked. We have learned from internal audit, accounts, legal, purchasing, sales, engineering, IT and many other managers. If you ask them to help you understand your role and how you can help them support it better, you are likely to find that they will reciprocate. They may be happy to make presentations to your people about their needs and their professional knowledge, and all of these interactions help in the quest to optimise the whole system.

External sources of stimulus, support, training and development
Why paid-for help will be needed

No organisation can possibly employ all of the skills it needs. This would be like a general medical practitioner doing brain surgery, or an infantry regiment making its own boots. Successful organisations evolve to know which skills they should employ, which specialisms (such as transport, perhaps) they should contract with continually, and which organisations (property advisers, for example) they should have on call for the occasions when they are needed.

It is hard to generalise about which of these resources or services should be permanently employed and which contracted. Success can be found in contrasting styles as, for instance, an IT company which may be hardware-based such as Dell, software-based such as Microsoft, or integrated such as Apple. All have been extremely successful at different times, and each has completely different relationships with service providers.

Even such basic services as catering may be outsourced by some organisations or internal in others. The decisions should be based upon what the organisation is trying to accomplish on behalf of its customers, staff and shareholders, not on generalised formulae.

> It's impossible to be the best without being different.
> **Anon**

Your requirements for a consultant or training organisation will change as the transformation proceeds, so you need to know that possible providers will evolve and adapt. At first there will be some high pressure but limited scope of work to establish the programme and prove the concept. If this is successful there is likely to be an increased demand for both training and support. This will reduce eventually but leave a continuing requirement for routine training and programme support. Coaching of individual senior managers is important for the duration of the programme, as the demands upon them change at each stage of the Pathway described in Chapter 9.

Key areas for support:

- *Developing a strategy and supporting its implementation.* This requires in-depth experience from the consultant in using the methodologies and tools at the top level, and of designing and managing programmes. You will need to work jointly on increasing the awareness of the unacceptability of the current situation, and in convincing the doubters of the realism of being much better. The success of the consultant in addressing these two aspects of increasing readiness to change will determine the depth of drive and support in the early parts of the journey. Support to the top team should be committed initially for a year or so with a rolling extension for twelve months, so that the management team have the confidence that the programme will be persisted with. You must also be prepared to listen to feedback that will not always be comfortable to hear.

- *Supporting the first critical projects.* These have to succeed and be seen to do so. They must use the new approach diligently, and leaders should be brought to recognise how the approach was instrumental in the success. This acts as proof of concept. An experienced external project facilitator will support the project leader and integrate the activities with the senior management work and the skills development, building this credibility. Later projects can use internally developed people and the external requirement should be reduced.

    Specialist skills in statistical or other analysis techniques may need to come from outside. It's usually more economical to pay the daily rate when you need it rather than invest in full-time staff who will only occasionally be needed for their specialism.

- *Developing skills.* All staff, from directors to first line operators, need to learn and apply the principles, methodologies and tools. This needs a broad cross-section of learning processes, from workshops to training courses to online programmes, and you should choose the external provider with this in mind. Initially they will deliver all of the work, but should be ready to cooperate with you in developing your own people to deliver the routine content if you wish. You should expect to continue with the provider for the duration of the programme, perhaps permanently, to deliver specialist training and to train your trainers.

● *Stimulating the later phases of the programme.* As described in Chapter 9, programmes tend to move in phases, from surges of achievement to pauses whilst people catch their breath. An experienced consultant will be able to help leaders recognise the symptoms of slowing down, and help break through the impasses that otherwise lead to stagnation.

Choosing a new consultant / trainer

Of all the activities in this book, appointing a new provider is one for which PDSA is most critical and least risky. Requesting several proposals in response to an invitation to tender is asking for trouble. a long-term programme cannot be defined usefully to the level of detail required. The process will be dominated by experts – in selling from them and purchasing in your own organisation – none of whom may be involved in the ongoing relationships. Instead, carry out some small-scale exploratory work with companies discovered through personal reference. Use this pilot work to build on your initial ideas. You will already be getting returns on your investment and developing relationships that will benefit all.

Managing your consultant / trainer

Relationships between clients and their providers are rarely as constructive as they need to be. In earlier lives as senior managers we were involved with external consultants many times. We found that individual relationships were often strong, but that the contractual relationships between the companies were fraught. As clients we obtained benefits, but it often seemed that they were far below the potential that could have been achieved. And top managers often seemed to fail to understand the purpose of the consultancy, undermining the efforts to shift behaviours by refusing to release staff and not personally attending events that would have helped them understand.

The following guide points will help you optimise the relationships with your providers, and maximise the benefits from their expertise.

- *Clarify what you are trying to accomplish.* This should go without saying by this stage, but keep the Three-Question Model to the fore in all your discussions.

- *Work jointly to diagnose the organisation and agree a strategy.* Using the diagnosis process as described in Chapter 2 will build shared understanding and commitment. Any self-respecting consultant should require that they start with diagnosis, so the more you can involve yourself with this the stronger will be the relationship. Be ready to be challenged!

- *Think hard about your culture.* You need a consultant who fits to some extent, but not too much. They need to be sufficiently similar so that people feel they understand, whilst being sufficiently experienced and independent-minded to give unpalatable feedback when appropriate.

- *Avoid the complexity of a 'contract' if possible.* Agree rules of initial engagement; refine them as your relationship develops. Any written contract you develop will only be called for when the relationship has failed, so working principles are much easier to understand and use. One detail that is worth defining is the actions to be taken in the event of cancellation of events, so that all can be clear about the costs in advance.

- *Use the consultant's independence.* You are paying for their expertise and knowledge, their wide experience and the fact that they don't depend upon you for their living. Ask for advice and think hard before rejecting it; they are the ones most likely to shock you out of the habits which have led to the problems you are experiencing.

- *Be prepared to pay for client management time from the consultant.* You can expect a certain amount of 'free' time from their client manager as part of the benefit of the overall contract, as with any other service you may buy. However, they need to spend time on planning and reviewing with their people and with your management team, and you should agree a monthly amount to cover this. It will greatly enhance the robustness of the overall effort.

- *Use their standard training curriculum and processes first.* These have been developed over many years and presumably work well or the company would not still be trading. Your company may, of course, have style guidelines and you may be prepared to pay for the conversion of handouts and visuals if this is felt to be sufficiently important. However, you should wait until the first round of projects and training are complete before insisting on customising their content and process. This is expensive to develop and unless there is some approach that is deeply rooted and demonstrably effective (in which case you probably don't need a new training provider) the expense may not be worthwhile.

- *Don't work on a payment by results basis.* This is a contentious issue. In the late eighteenth century James Watt sold his steam engines to mine owners by accepting a proportion of the coal saving as a fee. Many then refused to pay because the savings were so high they felt they had been deceived!

  In our field it can seem attractive to a client to mitigate the cost of consultancy by offering to pay a percentage of the gains as the fees. Indeed, with one large client we remember a project saving over a billion dollars; we would ourselves have been very happy to be on a gain-sharing deal. However, in our experience gain sharing is never satisfactory, mainly because of the potentially huge sums involved and the difficulty of allocation of credit. Success always has many parents. We would expect a well-founded project to return more than ten times its investment, but the costs of counting that gain to sufficient precision to justify a cheque are more than can be justified. In addition, many of the gains are not cash gains, or are perhaps deferred, or may be capital rather than revenue.

  However, it is still very important that you keep track of the expenditure on your providers and the costs incurred inside the business on the one hand, and agree the benefits with your finance colleagues on the other hand. You should then use this balance sheet at programme reviews, both internally and with the consultants. A good programme will be self-funding, but don't waste too much effort on the fine details.

- *Make long-term commitments and expect continuity.* It's important that you and your people build relationships with the consultants and trainers, and they will recognise this. The further ahead you can arrange your schedules the more you can ensure that you get the people you want allocated to your work.

- *Develop strategies but don't over-define the detail.* The very nature of the transformation process is that it will need to focus on learning, adapting to the experience of the particular circumstances. There's certainly going to be a need for major effort for years, but anything further out than six months needs to be flexible enough to respond to the needs as they emerge. This makes budgeting difficult, but demanding a month-by-month spend too far out will distort the process and become arbitrary.

- *Make sure you engage with their senior consultant.* Smaller companies tend to have more mature consultant / trainers, with the benefits of working experience. Their owners will know all of their staff and have insights on options that make them more effective. You should look for evidence that they have developed a standardised service, able to provide you with consistency.

- *Keep track of spend and benefits.* As mentioned above, you must understand and publicise the balance sheet of the programme. No matter how much the gains accumulate, as the transformation develops you will find that some top managers increase their resistance when their own behaviour comes into question. The very least you can do is to make sure that the top team has experienced the project and programme reviews, and that they know what is different, why it is different, what the costs and gains have been.

- *Recognise the potential benefits of the provider's continuity.* In most organisations there is a constant turnover in internal trainers and change agents – they move on to other jobs or leave the business. This means that the improvement programme can forget its roots and lose the attention to principles and detail that was part of the original success. It is routine for us to allocate a trainer or consultant to a client who was working with them ten years before, and this supports credibility of claims to be mounting a consistent long-term effort.

Organising help, in relation to the System of Profound Knowledge

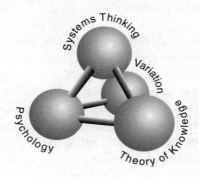

Check at every stage that you have considered each component, looking for insight and consistency on behalf of your own understanding.

Systems thinking:
- Explore the connections and influences across the whole system.
- Study the various aims, visions and missions of other organisations, and listen to how they inspire (or don't inspire) their leaders and staff.
- Integrate the consultants and trainers into your system, to maximise the contribution they can make, for instance by their trainers being aware of and supporting current initiatives.

Variation:
- Search for examples of how 'on target with minimum variation' helped an organisation to improve by comparison with 'work to specification'.

Theory of knowledge:
- All of these explorations and subsequent applications should follow PDSA: we have found that this model becomes more powerful as the years go by.

Psychology:
- You will find many kindred spirits in other organisations, so be ready to be as much help to them as they are to you.
- Keep your boss aware of the possibilities for both them and/or senior colleagues to make visits, attend conferences, and so on.

In conclusion...

We recognise that it is still rare for all of the elements described in this book to be fully implemented – the default way of life. However, we have seen every ingredient make its contribution, sometimes combining to make spectacular gains. Our colleagues and clients have experienced many epiphanies, and once that has happened they become committed for life.

The reasons for the limited scale of long-term application are many, and we have touched on some of them, short-term financial or other targets, and linking them to pay being a major culprit. But beyond these and other logical barriers is the unfortunate truth that once you have obtained a senior position acting in a particular way, it generally looks much safer to carry on with what made you successful rather than taking risks with new ways in which you are not practised.

Work with those who do want to take the chance on changing themselves, and the risks are actually minimal if they commit to the approach, using the methodologies we have described to guide the tools, in the context of PDSA. As we asserted earlier, the principles are sound, the methods logical and the tools are honest.

We hope this book will get into the hands of young people, in ordinary jobs, who are perhaps only managing themselves. Once practised and when they have become familiar the tools can be relied upon for the rest of a working life, even as the scope and responsibilities increase as a consequence of success.

Appendix 1 Some history

Curiosity is more important than knowledge.
Albert Einstein, physicist, 1879–1955

This appendix provides some background into the never-ending processes of increasing our knowledge, hopefully linking to increasing your desire to learn more.

Developing our curiosity

Even though you have finished the main part of the book, you will almost certainly have more questions now than you had when you started it. Whilst your knowledge has increased, so too has your awareness of what you don't know. If this is so, you share the realisations of countless people over the centuries who have used and developed the scientific method as the basis of their learning.

The scientific method has revolutionised the way we have learned about the natural world over the last five hundred years or so, and this knowledge has been applied in countless ways to develop technologies and societies that our ancestors could never have conceived. It has only been adapted for use in leading and managing human organisations in the last few decades, and those who are taking advantage of it are realising benefits that are also beyond anyone's expectations.

Having said that, science and the scientific method are neither infallible nor do they produce only beneficial outcomes, of course. They are ways to help humans think more clearly, and are as subject to human frailty (and even malevolence) as are other philosophies. It is up to the user to apply them to benefit humankind.

Explaining cause and effect is a good start

The first step in learning lies in being able to explain a cause and effect system, and using that tentative explanation (hypothesis) to make predictions. This puzzle goes back to the dawn of human consciousness and there is still much that is fascinating in the thoughts of Greek philosophers. A quote from the polymath Aristotle (384–322BC) is useful for any manager: 'Observing the world gives us an idea of the problems that exist'. This is why we must start PDSA with Study – study of the actual work rather than just the data, numeric or otherwise.

However, other ancient philosophers had a quite different approach. For many centuries 'learning' was dominated by abstract thinking rather than observing, and with interpretation of ideas of perfection, regardless of what people experienced. The philosophic world looked down on those who observed. 'Practical' people could in turn be quite disdainful of philosophers.

This attitude held back learning about the realities of the natural world for over a thousand years. 'Truths' or axioms ruled, and scholars confined themselves to interpreting these foundations. This approach is called deduction. Evidence that did not fit was not wanted.

Slowly, through the fifteenth and sixteenth centuries in Europe, people started to ask questions about what they were experiencing. This could be fatally risky if they challenged the established explanations, particularly if they had been incorporated into religious texts.

The English philosopher, statesman and author Francis Bacon (1561–1626) is widely credited with the describing idea of the scientific method as we know it today. He wrote of the value of 'Observe when [something happens], and when not. Observe how much?' This simple mantra remains a useful way to approach any situation, and again underpins our recommendation to start the PDSA cycle with Study. Bacon was a great experimenter, and indeed he died by not considering the consequences of trying to freeze a chicken. (He should have done some contingency analysis!)

Observation can be revolutionary when used to generate new hypotheses and theories

The astronomer Galileo (1564–1642), Bacon's contemporary, also observed – through the telescope he invented – and saw what he correctly interpreted as moons orbiting Jupiter. Prior authorities had held it axiomatic (i.e, 'true') that the Earth was the centre of the universe and thus all bodies including the sun must orbit it (as, of course, they appear to do to the naked eye). During the previous hundred years or so, observations and calculations by the early astronomer Copernicus (1473–1543) and then by Kepler (1571–1630) had shown many inconsistencies with ancient earth-centred models, but their writings were extremely hard for non-mathematicians to follow and so could be ignored by those who didn't want to know. (They were seen as 'just hypotheses'.) Galileo had been in correspondence with Kepler, but hadn't so far been vocal in support of his model that put the sun at the centre of the solar system.

Galileo's approach is called 'induction': using evidence from observation, in this case of the solar system, to develop a new conclusion. It was clear to him that if an observation showed that one thing contradicted the axiom – that the earth is at the centre of the cosmos – then the whole basis of the axiom was questionable and probably wrong, no matter how hard any authority denied it. That just made them wrong too – a life-threatening thing to accuse the authorities of at that time, and which is still pretty risky in many organisations today.

Galileo also carried out experiments, trying out ideas on a small scale to see if his ideas (hypotheses) worked out in practice. They became robust theories as a result of the accumulation of data that supported them. He constantly undermined axioms that were asserted to be true by authority figures regardless of the evidence. He went further, however. He would not allow his sun-centred model to be classed as a 'theory', but insisted that anyone who did not accept it to be true was stupid – including, or even especially, the Pope. Galileo spent years under house arrest as a consequence.

Any manager involved with change and improvement will sometimes find themselves in Galileo's position. Their organisation will be influenced by countless policies derived from past beliefs about how things are. Some of these beliefs and policies will still be valid, others outdated. Some top managers will feel possessive about some of them and neutral about others. The manager adopting the process-management approach in this book does not believe what they are told; they go and see instead. They carry out tests that might come to different conclusions to the ones in the policies and then discover that if they do, the top managers may not like these conclusions and disbelieve the evidence. We suggest that the change agent goes carefully at this stage; the modern organisational equivalent of Galileo's house arrest is to lose your job. Hence the many references to working on increasing readiness to change throughout this book.

This scientific approach has not won universal acceptance. Most of our lives today is dominated by policies and politics deduced from axioms that no one seems able to demolish regardless of the evidence. For instance, that performance-related pay is a good thing. That private company management is good; public management is bad. Private investment is good; public investment is waste. And many more. Few people in positions of power will listen to evidence to see that a policy is sometimes good, sometimes bad, and that therefore it needs to be refined (by testing using PDSA) rather than reimposed. Indeed, most politicians are resistant to carrying out experiments in order to test their ideas.

Scientists came to realise that a process combining thought and experiment, deduction and induction, worked really well in coming up with theories that could reliably predict into new circumstances. You can start with general idea (theory), deducing the expectation of particular events, then from the observation of those events inducting back to the theory that might need modification if the events were surprising.

Small-scale experiments can help to understand whole systems

Sir Isaac Newton (1642–1727) developed the concept combining the experiment further. If you can look at how things work on a very small scale, for instance sunbeams through a prism in a dark room, you can come to new conclusions about the very large scale, in this case the properties of light that is produced by the sun. This is amazing when you think about it, and seems to have been very controversial at the time.

Newton laid out four rules of scientific reasoning:

1. It must be about discovering causes which are true.
2. The same effects must be shown to come from the same causes.
3. The explanations must be constant and universal.
4. Hypotheses that merely explain history are not useful. Useful hypotheses are predictive and validated by experience.

These rules were adopted with great enthusiasm by the natural philosophers of the seventeenth and eighteenth centuries (the term 'scientist' was not introduced until the nineteenth century). You will recognise that they underpin the enquiries and tests we have described in the PDSA Cycle.

Newton is regarded as a crucial figure in the development of scientific philosophy, but some of his theories have nonetheless had to be modified, overtaken by precision of measurement or extremes of circumstance. His theories of gravity stood the test of more than two hundred years of application, and only came to be challenged when measurement technology improved. Einstein showed that under the extreme conditions of physics near the speed of light, Newton's calculations do not work well enough. This does not make Newton 'wrong' – his physics still sufficed to put landing craft on the moon – but new theories are more useful in extreme circumstances such as when applied close to the speed of light or in the atomic nucleus.

This remains a universal concept: old theories that have been useful are always vulnerable to different circumstances, or to new, or more accurate, data. All of us need to be aware of this when we are tempted to ignore data that seem to contradict our long-held beliefs.

In everyday life there's too much to keep our eyes on

What should we observe? Finding useful data can itself be difficult; there's an infinite amount to see. Just try noticing everything that's going on in the high street next time you drive down it and you will see that normally you are filtering out almost everything that is happening except those factors relevant to you, as the driver. But be careful: if by any chance you filter out the wrong things you might cause an accident or drive through a red light.

The Scottish philosopher David Hume (1711–76) proposed that observation must be carried out within a context: it's no good just looking about and recording everything you see. You would be overwhelmed by junk data (as indeed managers often are, people having forgotten why some data were ever collected). Observing with no context will thus not lead to learning. For our purposes one will not go far wrong by using the System of Profound Knowledge to guide one's initial Study of an organisation.

If any of these points seem like common sense, beware. They have become familiar to many of us because of our education, but many people do not discipline their observations, and critical things can be going on that they miss – remember the trees falling in the forest with nobody hearing them. It's not that people don't have their eyes open; they have not thought about what they should be looking out *for*. If they are concentrating on meeting the cost targets it's likely that the customer (or patient, student, claimant) experience will be ignored.

To be valid, a theory must be capable of falsification

In the mid-twentieth century, the philosopher Karl Popper (1902–94) asserted that science should be about trying to construct the most robust theories by deliberately experimenting to disprove hypotheses, looking for contrary evidence. If a theory cannot be tested to failure it is not likely to be useful. For instance, a new medical theory is double-blind tested: half the subjects *and their doctors* don't know whether they are taking the real medication or a placebo. This is widespread practise in the academic world, and is the principal reason why those new theories that do survive are usually very robust indeed. Anything that survives a peer-reviewed double-blind test is pretty likely to be useful. It is, however, rare in business. Which top manager wants their ideas exposed to efforts to disprove them? But it has been adopted to some extent and is the philosophy behind Toyota's requirement for suppliers to run a supposedly improved process with the supposed improvement taken out. If the problem does not reappear, the solution is not valid.

All data is subject to uncertain accuracy in itself and in its measurement

Werner Heisenberg (1901–76), the German theoretical physicist, made another disconcerting assertion with his Uncertainty Principle: that one can never establish both the speed and the location of an electron, one can only predict to a degree of probability. Such probable predictions are an essential component of applied nuclear physics, such as satnavs and so on, but Einstein went to his grave dissatisfied with the concept – he never stopped trying to find certainty. So, clever though he undoubtedly was, Einstein could be wrong too.

Any manager asserting the definiteness of some data is likely to be found out to be wrong. Especially in budgeting!

In the 1920s and 30s, the American physicist and statistician Walter Shewhart (1891–1967) realised that uncertainty applied to measures in work processes, and built on probability thinking to discriminate between noise (common cause variation) and signals (assignable, or special cause variation) in the data. This idea is the basis of Statistical Process Control, enabling us to tell the difference between an abnormality and a failure. W E Deming, Kaoru Ishikawa and others evolved their way to the PDCA (Plan Do Check Act) cycle in the 1950s, via various intermediate stages from Shewhart's original circle that incorporated these statistical texts.

Attempts to apply science to management are very recent

F W Taylor (1856–1915), an American mechanical engineer, promoted 'scientific management' in the early twentieth century. He did carry out experiments, but was remarkably constrained by axioms around the 'fact' that workers could have no role to play in using their intelligence. This seriously limited the applicability of any learning and gave the term 'scientific management' such a bad name that it is still only just recovering.

To summarise: starting with the general idea of the System of Profound Knowledge, deduce the aspects of the system worth observing. From the observation of how the work works in the selected area, induct some general theories of cause and effect, and evaluate these theories using PDSA to guide experiments. Then apply the learning to make the work work better.

There are thus less than a hundred years of attempts to apply the power of science to leading organisational change. We have experienced nearly half of that in time terms, and have a big exposure to the efforts of the last forty-plus years.

Plan Do Study Act – The Deming Cycle

In our practice and travels we have seen and experienced many approaches to learning and improvement. We did not start out with PDSA as an axiom; in fact, we probably underplayed it early in the 1990s. The reason why this little model is so powerful is that sits on the shoulders of the giants described above and many more: hundreds of years of learning thinking and doing.

Why 'Study' and not 'Check?' As described, PDSA was developed (as Plan Do Check Act) in the late 1940s by Deming and Shewhart.

There is some debate about the difference between 'Check' and 'Study'. Deming originally used 'Check', but in the late 80s he changed it to 'Study' in response to its widespread misuse – in the West the word 'Check' was being interpreted as having a quick look to see if things were OK and then moving on to the next problem. This was not what was intended, and was certainly not the attitude of the better Asian companies for whom English was not the first language. 'Study' is clearly what Shewhart, Deming and the other founding fathers meant by 'Check' – so we have always used PDSA.

Appendix 2: Practice

Everyday performance revolution

After the theory, the practice. If you feel in tune with the book, here's what you need to get used to doing, everyday.

1. Open the loop.
Develop theories that arise from the Study. Share these with at least one other person to see if they make sense.

2. Loop the loop.
Carry out experiments, involving others and on a small scale, as rapidly as possible, as many times as needed, to see if your theory holds water. Share your conclusions to see if they make sense.

3. Close the loop.
Implement, being ready to adapt if it now turns out there's not as much sense in your theory as you originally thought. And carry on studying, ready for the theory to become not so useful. Each cycle becomes another link in a chain of applied logic, showing explicit connections between exploration and implementation.

In this way you can make more rapid decisions, at lower risk, and see the work working better, faster at every stage.

Actions from Chapter 1. Find out how the work is working

	Observations
Observe the actual processes.	
Construct a map of your function within the wider organisation.	
Map the actual flow of key processes.	
Listen to what people think they are trying to accomplish – overall and in their own role.	
Identify the data they use for reporting and decision making.	
How do people distinguish between abnormalities and problems?	
Assess the levels of knowledge and competence.	
Remember that correlation of events is not the same as causation.	

Actions from Chapter 2. What should be happening?

Observations	
Experience what your customers experience.	
Listen to the customers' voices, especially those of demanding users.	
Understand the financial goals.	
Explore other goals.	
Establish some results measures that correlate with the goals.	
Make a first attempt at a diagnosis.	
Use meeting management processes systematically.	

Actions from Chapter 3. Trying out some changes

Observations	
Uncover hidden assumptions about trials, tests of theories.	
Gather the best team you can.	
Clarify the appropriate decision-making style for the circumstances.	
Generate some theories.	
Try some changes.	
Collect clean data.	

Actions from Chapter 4. Making sense of the results

Observations	
Clarify the principles of meeting for study rather than judgement.	
Be diligent with meeting management processes.	
Develop a good communication process, and test it.	
Review the improvement / trial process as well as its outcomes.	
Appreciate the team members and other contributors.	

Actions from Chapter 5. Implementing improvements

Observations	
Be explicit about theories of implementation in this environment.	
Involve process owners if relevant.	
Use and explain the process management cycle.	
Develop sensible standard operating procedures.	
Develop decent display boards for the launch.	

Actions from Chapter 6. Managing ongoing performance

Observations	
Generate a routine for visiting the actual work.	
Develop open, process-oriented questions to focus conversations.	
Understand the details of standard operations, to ensure they haven't descended into bureaucracy.	
Organise your own workplace and habits to be an example to others.	

Actions from Chapter 7. Dealing with problems

Observations	
Develop your people in order to know how to respond to problems quickly and calmly, even when they are on their own.	
Be open with your boss, colleagues and staff when incidents have happened.	
Be systematic about developing explicit theories of upstream causes.	

Actions from Chapter 8. Improving on a larger scale

Observations	
Confirm / ensure that the projects are carefully prioritised according to the organisation's strategy.	
See that the right people are in place as sponsors, leaders and facilitators.	
See that support is properly organised and budgeted for.	
Witness gateway reviews, to ensure that they are being conscientiously run and generating good learning.	
See that end of project reports are properly written up and the conclusions shared.	

Appreciations

I owe thanks to many people over the years. Some for ideas, some for opportunities, others for sharing their knowledge; some at a distance, as an inspiration or as teachers, and others close to, in dialogues that worked away at concepts until they became real.

Jane Seddon comes first, co-owner of PMI for many years, and co-author of *Working with the Grain*, first published in 2009. Coming from an educational background, Jane had also encountered Dr Deming in his later years and been inspired by his concepts and humanity as I was. She brought knowledge and practice in the educational and interpersonal field, including leading a management college, to add to my business and commercial experience. Her insights into the challenges and opportunities faced by top managers and her support have been inspirational and a privilege to witness. We have worked together with numerous clients, progressively refining many of the models used in this book, and using them with teams and individuals. In most cases I am not sure which of the ideas are hers, which mine.

Practical methods need testing by application if they are to be robust, and the strength of my assertions through the book is based upon much practice, as you might hope. Amongst those who I would like to thank for providing environments that supported this include bosses and clients over more than thirty years: John Corbett, Tony Coles, Estelle Clarke, Peter Mathis, John Clothier, Alan Curtis, Paul Jennings, Joe Cullen, Anthony Robinson, Lee Ryant, Bill Holland, Frank Hayden, Norman Hardie, Peter Collins, Bob Morley, Ian Hau, Bob Parker, Søren Laungaard and Lucas Vos. There have also been clients and bosses whose intransigence and eccentricity forced me, in both employment and consulting, to develop ways of moving forward in guerrilla style without them noticing at first. It's better they don't feature by name here. But, in fact, without this aggravation – which led us to develop methods that engage managers in difficult circumstances – the whole approach would be much less powerful. You can't wait for everyone to be ready to change before starting.

The field of 'quality management' is open and cooperative in sharing its learning, and it has been a privilege to work with thinkers and practitioners around the world. A particular pleasure has been the annual meetings of what we have called the Global Quality Futures Workshop, which has its origins in discussions with Dr Deming in the late 80s. As well as ourselves, members consist of a small number of Japanese, American and Indian academics, consultants and managers. It has proven a fruitful forum for validating our ideas with some of the world's leading thinkers and hearing about global applications. Through this route and others, many fellow professionals over the years have been generous with their knowledge and insights, in particular Noriaki Kano, Tom Johnson, Henry Neave, Tom Nolan, Lloyd Provost, Ron Moen, Elaine Johnson, Yoshinori IIzuka, N (Ram) Ramanathan and John Pearson.

The founder of PMI in the USA, Lou Schultz, took a risk in 1990 by supporting Colin Nichols in appointing me to PMI in the UK. Subsequently he worked with Jane and me to enable us to take over in the UK, initially as a franchise and, later on, completely. Amongst many US PMI staff, Keith Setterholm, John Vollum, Roger Longbotham and John Persico persisted in helping this Managing Director take the first steps into becoming a consultant.

I would also like to thank those who took the trouble to comment in detail on my drafts. James Horton, J Ravikant (Ravi) and Peter Goodliffe, provided comments as the chapters emerged, and I have been glad to incorporate many of their refinements. My colleagues Martyn Tebb, Warren Knight, Rebecca Seddon and Richard Seddon read the whole book, and again I have been glad to adopt many suggestions. It is sobering to think that this consultation and adaption process might go on forever, but one has to draw a line somewhere.

And thanks also to those who encouraged me to keep going whilst writing – especially my wife Penny, my publisher Richard Burton and Susannah Clarke – during the tough times when much is done, but there is still so much to have to persist with.

Regardless of this help, the opinions in the book, as well as any errors and omissions, are mine. Do let me know if you find any errors; it's really hard to guarantee none amongst 60,000 or so words!

Ann

I am aware of the possibilities of exaggeration when presenting illustrations to support a principle, but all of Ann's exploits and incidents are based on reality – some of them toned down! Indeed, through the years of interactions with colleagues, customers, suppliers, clients and so on our constant refrain has been 'you couldn't make this up!'. Such never-ending drama has sated any appetite I might have had for soap operas, and there are many other tales probably too tall to be believed.

Evolving models and ideas

Those who follow PMI's work may notice some variations in the details of wording and graphics compared with what they have seen before. A book is a broadcast medium trying to convey concepts with words and pictures. These are often poor substitutes for the thoughts in each of our heads, and particularly so in comparison with practice and dialogue. Thus, even when writing about the same concept one is constantly trying new ways of getting to the ideas.

Dr Deming sometimes made a point of declaring that he was presenting something in a new way, either as a result of his own thinking changing, or thanks to a new contribution from a collaborator. Hence his book *The New Economics*, written at the age of 91, contained modifications to aspects of his book *Out of the Crisis* – written when he was 83!

So please bear with us if you find something not quite the same as you have seen it before. It probably does not mean that the previous graphic or description was 'wrong'; it's that I thought a different approach might be more appropriate for a particular circumstance. Meanwhile, the essentials have definitely not changed. Over more than twenty years we have found the System of Profound Knowledge, and PDSA in particular, complete and necessary in order to make work work better.

About PMI

Process Management International

PMI is unusual in the world of business improvement consultancy and training in basing our practice on explicit theoretical foundations – in our case Dr Deming's System of Profound Knowledge. The company was founded in 1984 to build upon Dr Deming's approach and has continually developed programme, consulting and training services to put his theories (and others) into operation for the benefit of clients wishing to achieve better results. We have always collaborated with academics and practitioners, initially in Japan, and later across the US and UK, in developing an unmatched breadth and depth of support and learning materials.

In that time, the business has helped many organisations with their improvement programmes and served thousands of people through its in-house, public and web-based services. As partners of the UK's Chartered Quality Institute, the oldest such body in the world, PMI offer services and support that achieve rapid, effective and permanent results.

Today our headquarters are in the UK, and we work with clients around the world. We are proud of our relationships dating back to the 1980s, and people tell us that our special appeal is our combination of logical process analysis with key aspects of interpersonal and cultural behavioural change. These help them to address their organisational challenges, thereby enabling them to make effectiveness and efficiency gains that have collectively amounted to several billion US dollars. But in addition to that, and the reason why people remember their encounters with us for so long, our approach is rewarding personally and emotionally, enabling them to make sense of their work – and of their future.

Process Management International

www.pmi.co.uk
Villiers Court, Birmingham Road,
Meriden Business Park, Meriden, CV5 9RN
Tel: +44 (0)1676 522766
Email: info@pmi.co.uk

Jan Gillett

Following a degree in Geology in 1968, Jan Gillett joined the Pilkington Group in Lancashire, England, where he cut his teeth in sales, product and market development, and became customer service manager for the Fibreglass division in 1980. Here he led the function though a major technology change and sponsored quality circle teams, amongst the first in the UK in administrative functions. In 1983 he was appointed Managing Director of the Pilkington subsidiary Kitsons Insulation Products Limited, a merchant with fifteen branches across the UK.

In 1986 he become Managing Director of Sketchley Textile Services Ltd, which manufactured, managed and laundered work wear to 500,000 people across UK industry and commerce. It was in this role that he responded to the invitation of their major customer Ford Motor to take up Deming's approach to Total Quality Management. He led the consequent company-wide transformation across ten locations and 2,000 people, meeting Dr Deming several times during this work. He also sponsored a division to achieve the BS5750 Quality Standard.

Jan Gillett took on the challenge of establishing PMI, then US owned, in the UK from 1990. He became a Director of the British Deming Association, and also Chair of the Alliance of Deming Consultants. Attending several of Dr Deming's famous Four-Day Seminars, he provided contingency cover for Deming's last event in Europe, in Zurich in 1993.

Together with Jane Seddon, from the mid 1990s, he bought the UK PMI business from the Americans and led its development in working with clients in every sector, and in every continent.

Jan Gillett is a Fellow of the Chartered Management Institute and a Member of the Chartered Quality Institute. He has also been a non-executive director in several organisations, helping them rethink their strategies and policies to adjust to changing circumstances. He has presented at many conferences across Europe, Asia and the United States, and is a visiting lecturer to the University of Warwick's Manufacturing Group.

Further study

Many shelves of books line the business section of any large bookstore. We have found the following stimulating and useful.

Making Your Work Work complements *Working with the Grain*, Gillett J., Seddon J. (2012, second edition), Process Management International 978-0-954605-6-5. We describe the principles and challenges of organisational transformation, and explore programmes to help make a success of it. In particular, we explore parallels between our approach and the field of Natural Systems thinking.

ABOUT DR DEMING

W Edwards Deming Institute: www.deming.org is the official site for the man, his history and current activities about his approach.

Out of the Crisis, Deming, W. E. (2000, second edition), MIT Press. 978-0262541152
Deming's definitive work from the mid 1980s. Open it at any page and you will find valuable insights. Although it is inevitably inclined towards the US in the 1980s, it remains highly relevant.

The New Economics, Deming, W. E. (2000, second edition), MIT Press. 978-0262541169
Originally published in the year of his death, this book is an easier read and contains his explanation of the System of Profound Knowledge.

The Deming Management Method, Walton, M. (1992), Mercury Business Books. 978-1852521417
An accessible guide to putting Deming's ideas into practice in terms of 1980s culture.

The Deming Dimension, Neave, H. (1989), SPC Press. 978-0-945320-36-4
Another narrative of thinking and applications of Dr Deming's concepts, from the point of view of a British author.

SYSTEMS THINKING

Profit Beyond Measure, Johnson, H. T. and Broms, A. (2000), Prentice Hall. 978-0684836676

Tom's personal exploration of the implications for top managers in accepting the lessons from Toyota, and transforming towards more emphasis on how things are done as opposed to only thinking about targets and results.

Fifth Discipline, The, Senge, P. M. (2006, second edition), Random House Business Books. 978-1905211203

Peter Senge's classic work from the early 1990s updated and still just as relevant. More insight into how systems work. The companion *Field Guide* is packed with useful methods.

The Toyota Way, Liker, J. (2004), McGraw Hill. 978-0071392310

One of several books from Jeffrey Liker outlining Toyota's practices for anyone to use. Others include analysis of technical development and of training.

Toyota Kata, Rother, M. (2009), McGraw-Hill. 978-0-07-163523-3

Another insight into Toyota, with many useful guidelines. Toyota's problems in recent years do not lessen the validity of *The Toyota Way*: the problems have emerged from not being consistently rigorous with it.

The Universe Story, Swimme, B. and Berry, T. (1992) Harper Collins. 0062508350

Including an exploration of the Natural Systems principles. Much more to explore at http://www.thomasberry.org

Goals Gone Wild: The Systematic Side Effects of Over-Prescribing Goal Setting, Ordóñez, L. D., Schweitzer, M. E., Galinsky, A. D., and Bazerman, M. H., Harvard Business School, and available from http://hbswk.hbs.edu/item/6114.html as a free download.

A remarkable demolition job on historic practice from one of the foremost institutional advocates.

VARIATION
Understanding Variation, Wheeler, D. J. (2000, second edition) SPC Press. 978-0945320531
This is a short and very accessible book. If you only read one book about variation, make this one it. There are plenty more from Don Wheeler.

THEORY OF KNOWLEDGE
As we have explored in this book, we see the PDSA Cycle as a practical manifestation of the scientific method. There is no shortage of books about science; the most accessible for most readers are ones that tell stories to illustrate the learning process. Any book or TV or radio programme about the Large Hadron Collider at CERN will have multiple references to the power of theories, experiments, predictions and falsifications.

Curiosity: How Science Became Interested In Everything, Ball, P. (2012), Vintage. 9780099554271
A remarkable history book. Curiously, he doesn't really cover science in leadership, but the lessons are there for us nonetheless.

The Faber Book of Science, Carey, J. (Ed.) (1995), Faber and Faber 0-571-16352-1
A collection of stories illustrating the use of science in understanding the natural world.

Contextual Teaching and Learning, Johnson, E. B. (2001), Corwin Press. 978-076197865
Elaine Johnson makes a fascinating exploration of the three Natural Systems Principles in the inspiring context of helping children learn.

PSYCHOLOGY
Many of the books we recommend integrate thinking about psychology into their message, but Alfie Kohn addresses the relevant aspects of the subject directly.

No Contest, Kohn, A. (1993, second edition), Houghton Mifflin. 978-0395631256
An entertaining look at many aspects of human motivation and how much of the practice in employment and families is entirely counter-productive. If you like this you will also like his book *Punished by Rewards.*

A Beginner's Guide to the Brain, Johnson, E. B. (2012), The Teaching and Learning Compact. 978-0-9830965-1-3
A brief and readable inspiring synthesis of the vast amount of new knowledge about the brain gained over the last few years.

Human needs and motivation: Abraham Maslow and Frederick Herzberg reported over fifty years ago that money was not the motivation for people's satisfaction in life once their basic needs were attended to. Much more about their original work, and studies that validate it over the decades, is available on the web under their names.

GUIDES FOR IMPROVEMENT AND MANAGEMENT PRACTITIONERS
Peter Scholtes wrote two complementary classics: *The Team Handbook,* (with others; 2003, third edition) Oriel. 978-1884731266, and *The Leader's Handbook,* (1998), McGraw Hill. 978-0070580282

The Improvement Guide, Langley, G. J., Moen, R., Nolan, K. M., Nolan, T. W. Norman, C. L and Provost, L. P. (1996), Jossey Bass. 978-0787902575
A formal, detailed reference book, based upon Deming's approach.

The Process Manager's Handbook, Gillett, J. and colleagues (2012, fourth edition), Process Management International 978-0954060527
PMI's summary of the principal methods and tools, and *The Project Leader's Handbook,* (2011), Process Management International 978-0-9540605-4-1 – our companion to *The Process Manager,* expanded to include many improvement project tools for teams and individuals.

Awards bodies
Deming Prize: www.juse.or.jp/e/deming
Malcolm Baldrige National Quality Award: www.baldrige.org
EFQM Excellence Award: www.efqm.org

Index